Th

WILLIAM SHAKESPEARE

www.pocketessentials.com

First published in Great Britain 2002 by Pocket Essentials, 18 Coleswood Road, Harpenden, Herts, AL5 1EQ

Distributed in the USA by Trafalgar Square Publishing, PO Box 257, Howe Hill Road, North Pomfret, Vermont 05053

Copyright © Ian Nichols 2002
Series Editor: Paul Duncan

A CIP catalogue record for this book is available from the British Library.

ISBN 1-904048-05-6

2 4 6 8 10 9 7 5 3 1

Book typeset by Wordsmith Solutions Ltd
Printed and bound by Cox & Wyman

Dedicated to every actor who has ever stumbled over the lines, every student who has wondered what the hell it all meant, and every director who has ever gone home and hit the gin bottle, but mostly to my wife, Susan, who had to put up with all the swearing.

CONTENTS

Introduction

It almost seems redundant to introduce William Shakespeare. His plays are the best-known and most produced in English, and it follows that he is the best-known playwright. Many of his plays have been in continuous production since they were written, and they have been filmed and televised more often than the works of any other. It would be difficult to find a person in any country of the English-speaking world who has not seen at least one play on stage or large or small screen. For better or worse, Shakespeare has formed the basis of literature courses at high schools and universities around the world, and his plays have provided the inspiration for films as diverse as *Forbidden Planet* and *Shakespeare In Love*. Lines from his plays and poems have crept into our daily discourse, even if they are often misquoted, and the number of stories with titles drawn from his work is far too numerous to count. It seems incredible that one man could have so much impact on our language and literature. So who was Shakespeare?

William Shakespeare was born on or about the 23 April 1564, the son of John Shakespeare, a glover, and Mary Arden. There is no record of his birth, but he was baptised on 26 April and would only have been a few days old. He was educated at grammar school and was, for a brief time, a country schoolmaster. Not all his time was spent teaching though for he made an older woman, Anne Hathaway, pregnant, and married her. His first child, Susanna, was born in 1583 and twins were born to him and Anne in 1585. Times were hard, his father's business was in the doldrums, and it is likely that he left soon after the twins were born to seek his fortune in London.

How he fell in with theatre people and what inspired him to begin writing is not known. It may simply be that he lived in Shoreditch when he came to London and the theatres were nearby. It may have been a chance meeting with such luminaries as Christopher Marlowe, who was his contemporary and already an established writer. Whatever the reason, his first play, *Henry VI, Part 1*, was written and performed in 1590. From then until his death on 23 April 1616, he wrote another 36 plays, four major poems and 154 sonnets. His last play was almost certainly *Henry VIII* in 1613. For the last three years of his life he retired to Stratford, although he visited London at least once a year to look after his financial interests in his company, originally the Lord Chamberlain's Men but then the King's Men. He and his partners built The Globe Theatre as a home for the company in 1599.

Shakespeare was the most popular dramatist of his day and grew wealthy enough to buy property back home in Warwickshire and to apply for a coat of arms. He had the patronage of Henry Wriothesly, the Earl of Somerset, and the friendship of many other lords and ladies. He was most certainly known to, and appreciated by, both Queen Elizabeth I and King James I. His poems were dedicated to Wriothesly, who had been of immense help to his career, particularly when the theatres were closed in 1592-3 due to the plague. *Venus And Adonis* was published in 1593 and *The Rape Of Lucrece* in 1594. *A Lover's Complaint* and the Sonnets were not published until 1609, although his last-written poem, *The Phoenix And The Turtle*, was published in 1601. None of his plays were ever published by him, nor were there any authorised editions in his lifetime. He earned his living from performances and did not want his plays available to anyone who wanted to perform them. There were quarto-sized volumes published but these were stolen and generally poor copies. It was not until the First Folio edition of 1623, published by Fleming and Condell, that his plays were gathered together and printed.

For centuries, people have wondered how the son of a Warwickshire glover, with only a grammar-school education, could have written plays and poetry which have affected the whole course of language and culture in English. Many alternatives have been suggested for the authorship, from the Earl of Oxford to Francis Bacon. It has been suggested that in the 'lost' years Shakespeare travelled extensively and gained experience. It has been suggested that the plays are, in fact, the work of many hands, and that the name was one simply used by the company for them all. All these suggestions are caused by the unwillingness to recognise a simple fact; one person can, in fact be responsible for such an effect, if that person possesses the genius for writing which belonged to William Shakespeare.

Plays

Henry VI, Part One (1590)

She's beautiful, and therefore to be wooed;
She is a woman, therefore to be won.

(Act v. Sc. 3.)

Story: The play revolves around the struggle for power which occurs after the death of Henry V. His son, Henry VI, is too young to take the throne, and English possessions in France are under threat from the armies led by Joan of Arc. With this lack of direct leadership from a king, civil war threatens between the Yorkists and Lancastrians, who have old grudges to settle, and these are symbolised by the red and white roses worn by the factions.

On assuming power, Henry VI tries to settle the differences between to two factions, but to no avail. A brawl in parliament between the Duke of Gloucester and the Bishop of Winchester presages the fighting and treachery to come, even though Henry achieves an agreement between them. When Henry leaves for France, the fragile peace between the lords falls apart.

Henry is crowned in France, but has to return to England to settle the infighting, hoping that Lord Talbot, the leader of his forces in France, can achieve victory over the French and Joan, now reinforced by the traitorous Duke of Burgundy. Talbot is betrayed by Richard, Duke of York, and is killed.

Richard captures Joan, and Suffolk, another lord, captures Margaret, the daughter of Reignier, an important French noble. Joan is executed, and Margaret and Henry are betrothed in an attempt to heal the breach between France and England. The wedding achieves a temporary peace but many lords aren't happy with this arrangement and the groundwork is laid for the events which follow in the next two plays.

Discussion: This is almost certainly the first of Shakespeare's plays. The story is straightforward and the complications of the brawling lords are truncated. It seems almost as if Shakespeare was feeling out the strategies he practised so well in later plays, wherein the action is more concentrated.

This play sprawls because it is a first play. Action takes place in a far wider compass than in later plays and the characters are drawn more laboriously. There are less of the truly memorable speeches but the dialogue is still inventive. It is as if Shakespeare was more concerned with getting the history right than creating memorable characters, as if he had not yet found the way to shape a whole history in a few words but had mastered all the mundane aspects of dialogue.

The character of Joan is interesting because she is portrayed as a witch with her victories due to demons. Her later beatification seems at odds with this. With her death, the Anglo-French marriage and the disgruntled nobles at the end of the play, the scene is set for further conflict in the best tradition of soap operas.

Background: Holinshed's *Chronicles* were the main source for the play but Shakespeare was undoubtedly influenced by Hall's *The Union Of The Two Noble And Illustrious Families Of York And Lancaster*.

Films: The BBC's 1983 version is available, which gives a serviceable reading of the play.

Verdict: Journeyman work, overwritten, with a certain stiffness to the long speeches but the sly details of courtly manipulation are beautifully done. 2/5

Henry VI, Part Two (1591)

The first thing we do, let's kill all the lawyers.

(Act iv. Sc. 2.)

Story: Henry's marriage to Margaret of France has caused disruption and dissatisfaction among the lords of England. There are plots to remove Henry from the throne and to replace him with Richard, the Duke of York. There are also plots against Humphrey, Henry's protector, by Cardinal Beaufort, and against Humphrey's wife, Elinor.

The plots against Humphrey and Elinor are successful—Humphrey is fired as Protector and Elinor banished. Margaret and Beaufort continue to plot against Humphrey and he is arrested for high treason. With the aid of Richard, they eventually succeed in having Humphrey killed.

As these plots run their course, the French take over the English possessions in France and Ireland rebels. This forces Henry to leave for France, and he sends Richard to put down the Irish rebellion, unaware of the part Richard played in Humphrey's death. The situation worsens when Jack Cade raises a revolt in England and the Commons demand to know the truth about the death of Humphrey. A succession of deaths among the lords further destabilises the situation and Cade takes London, defeating the king's armies, but his own forces turn on him when a huge reward is offered for his head.

Richard betrays Henry by bringing his troops back from Ireland and demanding the head of the Duke of Somerset, Henry's most faithful supporter. Somerset is confined to the Tower of London, but Margaret brings him out, and this gives Richard an excuse to break faith and go to war. He wins the battle, kills Somerset and is left the dominant power in the land, ready to challenge Henry in front of Parliament for the crown.

Discussion: A complex play. It's difficult to follow all the betrayals, murders, plots and trickery. The characters are straightforward, in some cases almost stereotypically so. Henry is a wimp, whose solution to problems is to ask everyone to be nice. Just about every character, including Margaret, has more testosterone than him. Richard is the star character, with more depth and cunning than all the rest put together.

The theme of church versus state, which emerged in the first part of this trilogy, is reinforced here with Beaufort's assistance in the murder of Humphrey. This is part of a long-running conflict that is mirrored in the history plays. The question of who is actually entitled to the crown is brought into sharp relief with Jack Cade's claim to it, which, he admits to the audience, he simply made up. Anyone, it seems, can claim the throne as long as they can muster a few men behind them. Henry's marriage to Margaret was ill-considered, politically motivated and foolish. He paid top dollar for her and got a very bad bargain. The lands he traded off for her sowed the seed of discontent which cost him his crown.

Even with its complexity, the play rattles along. Murder follows on betrayal follows on revolt, and Margaret's love affair adds spice to it all. Henry's dithering is almost comic and Jack Cade and his followers are definitely comic.

Background: Shakespeare took more liberties with Holinshed in this play. He packed the dialogue with inventions of his own, as well as drawing from Ovid and other sources.

Films: The 1983 BBC production is faithful, with some good performances, but unimaginative.

Verdict: A whirlwind of a play with much packed into it. 4/5

Henry VI, Part Three (1591)

A little fire is quickly trodden out;
Which, being suffered, rivers cannot quench.

(Act iv. Sc. 8.)

Story: Richard, the Duke of York, has taken over London and is challenging Henry's right to the crown. There are factions which support
both sides, and to avoid all-out war a deal is struck; Henry will keep the
throne until death, but then the succession passes to Richard and his
heirs. The deal, however, is not satisfactory to Henry's supporters or
Queen Margaret. She raises an army and attacks Richard and his sons,
taking him at Sandal Castle and beheading him. The Yorkist faction
eventually triumph, and divide up the country between the remaining
sons of Richard. Henry is sent to the Tower of London.

Richard's son, Edward, sends emissaries to France to gain the French
King's daughter in marriage. Margaret is in France, and conspiring
against both the marriage and Edward. However, while Warwick, his
emissary, is there, Edward marries Lady Jane Grey. The French King,
Lewis, is insulted, and Warwick rejects Edward, joining Lewis in an
expedition to take the throne from him. A series of betrayals and chang-
ing loyalties sees Edward lose the crown and Henry reinstated, but only
temporarily. After a further series of battles and betrayals, in which the
invading French forces are defeated, Margaret is captured, Warwick is
killed and Richard, the Duke of Gloucester, kills Henry in the Tower.

Edward is triumphant, sends Margaret back to France for ransom and
takes his place on the throne. England has achieved peace at the cost of
a great deal of blood but the land is still divided in loyalty.

Discussion: The outstanding character of the play is Richard, Duke
of Gloucester, who will later become Richard III. His hatred of Edward
is made plain as is his patience. He bides his time but is always a sinister figure in the background.

Edward is portrayed as a bullying animal but he is a strong king,
decisive and warlike, whereas Henry was indecisive and favoured

appeasement over battle. This strategy might have worked in a kinder age but not in fifteenth-century England.

Background: The trilogy was conceived and written as a set and probably performed in sequence.

Films: The BBC's 1983 film is sound, but lacks excitement, although this is a difficult play to adapt to the small screen.

Verdict: Too much to explain in the compass of a play, with too many tangled webs of deceit. 2/5

A Comedy Of Errors (1591)

Small cheer and great welcome makes a merry feast.

(Act iii. Sc. 1.)

Story: Aegeon, merchant of Syracuse, is in Ephesus without money. That doesn't just mean that he's unable to sample the delights of the town, but that he'll be executed because he doesn't have a thousand marks on him. It's fair, though, because that's how Syracuse treats the citizens of Ephesus. Aegeon is on a quest to find his long lost son. His wife had twin boys eighteen years ago and bought two other twin boys to be their servants, but there was the inevitable shipwreck and one son and one servant were separated from the other, as were mother and father. After thirty-three years, it has occurred to Aegeon to look for his wife and son and servant. He did have the thousand marks needed to ransom himself but it's with his son Antipholus and his servant Dromio. His story wrings the heart of the Duke of Ephesus but not enough to disregard the financial requirement.

Aegeon's stalwart companions are in town looking for lodgings, unaware that Aegeon is in trouble. They are also unaware that their long-lost siblings are resident in Syracuse. These are also called Antipholus and Dromio. What proceeds are strange meetings and mistaken identities, as masters and servants are separated and reunited, but not necessarily the right master and servant, as merchants bring goods to one brother, then expect the other brother to pay, and as wives and courtesans mistake identities. The Abbess of Ephesus, brought in to treat the supposedly possessed Antipholus (Aegeon's Antipholus), turns out to be Aemilia, Aegeon's long lost wife.

Eventually, all the players are brought together and all is resolved. The correct brothers are reunited with wives and courtesans, and Aemilia and Aegeon are back together. The duke decides not to execute Aegeon after all, and the entire extended family, with a slightly bemused duke in tow, trots off to have dinner at the abbey.

Discussion: There is very little story, as such, to this play. Rather, it is an extended vaudeville sketch, of the type that Abbott and Costello did so well on the silver screen. As knockabout comedy it is excellent, as light as a soufflé, with the various identity errors worked with panache into the script. It demonstrates Shakespeare's early mastery of comedy and one can just imagine the groundlings in The Globe rolling on the floor in laughter. It is a play where the comedy comes from the situations rather than from the dialogue. It works, and works well, with much scope for the actors to enrich the parts.

Background: It is Shakespeare's first comedy, and he took it from the Latin comedies he had studied at school, probably Plautus, combining his *Maenaechmi* with a scene from the same writer's *Amphitruo*. His own contribution is to double the twins, and double the fun, adding confusion to confusion.

Films: The 1983 BBC version starred Roger Daltry, in a classic piece of miscasting, but is very faithful to the play. The 1985 version, directed by Gregory Mosher and Thomas Woodruff, and starring the Flying Karamazov Brothers, is a much funnier adaptation, with the lines largely unchanged.

Verdict: It is fun, light, and fast paced. Whatever it lacks in subtlety, it more than makes up for in sheer pace, like a precursor to the Marx Brothers. 4/5

Titus Andronicus (1591)

> She is a woman, therefore may be woo'd;
> She is a woman, therefore may be won.

(Act ii. Sc. 1.)

Story: Titus is a Roman general who returns from the wars and incurs the enmity of Queen Tamora of the Goths when he sacrifices one of her sons. Saturninus, the Emperor, courts and wins Tamora. His brother Bassanius, seizes Lavinia, Titus' daughter, and marries her despite the protests of Titus. Although these protests anger the Emperor, he and Titus are eventually reconciled. Meanwhile Tamora plots revenge.

With the aid of Aaron, a Moorish general who becomes her lover, Tamora succeeds in having her sons kill Bassanius and rape Lavinia. The sons cut out Lavinia's tongue and cut off her hands to prevent Lavinia from naming them as the killers and rapists. Aaron and Tamora also succeed in implicating Titus' sons in the murder and they are executed. Aaron tricks Titus into cutting off his own hand in a futile attempt to save his sons—when his hand is delivered back to him along with the heads of his sons, Titus swears revenge.

After a time, Lavinia writes the names of her attackers in the dust with a staff, and Titus begins his campaign of revenge against them. Lucius, Titus' remaining son, raises an army to attack Rome and is summoned to talks with Saturninus. Tamora and her sons disguise themselves and go to Titus to discover his plans, but he tricks Tamora into leaving, then cuts the boys' throats in front of Lavinia. He attends the talks and completes his revenge by serving the brothers in a pie, then killing Lavinia and Tamora. Saturninus kills Titus and Lucius kills Saturninus, then becomes emperor. Aaron, who has been the instigator of much of the misery, is dragged off to be tortured to death.

Discussion: There's never a dull moment, and the dialogue is, at times, riveting. The revenge theme is obvious, as is the plot. This is not a subtle play. It is, however, Shakespeare's first tragedy, and it's a tragedy in the grand fashion. Just about every one of the main characters is dead by the end of the play.

The problem is that all the gore and death begin to pall after a while and the ending, which should be horrifying and tragic, becomes somewhat comic. Possibly the most poignant scene in the play is that where Lavinia works out, with the help of Lucius' young son and his schoolbooks, how to tell the world who raped her. After that, there is just too much grotesquerie.

Background: The play comes from Ovid and Seneca, particularly the latter's *Thyestes*. Thirteen corpses litter the stage in this play and that's without a single major battle. The Elizabethans must have loved it.

Films: Christopher Dunne's 1999 adaptation of the play is reasonably faithful to the original and very well made.

Verdict: A case of overkill. 1/5

Two Gentlemen Of Verona (1592)

That man that hath a tongue, I say, is no man,
If with his tongue he cannot win a woman.

(Act iii. Sc. 1)

Story: Valentine, one of the two gentlemen of the title, goes to Milan, leaving behind his best friend Proteus. Proteus is in love with Julia, and she returns his love but not before he is sent to Milan to join Valentine. Valentine has fallen in love with Silvia, the daughter of the Duke of Milan. Valentine shows a picture of Silvia to Proteus, who promptly forgets his love for Julia and falls in love with Silvia. Julia, in the meantime, is on her way to Milan, dressed as a boy.

Proteus informs the Duke of Valentine's plans, and Valentine is banished. He falls into the clutches of bandits but wins their sympathy and they take him in. The duke intends to marry Silvia to Sir Thurio, and employs Proteus to help in this. Proteus then employs the disguised Julia to help him.

The denouement of the play comes after Silvia leaves Milan to escape the attentions of Thurio and Proteus. With the bandits capturing first her, and then the duke and Sir Thurio, all the players are reconciled. Julia marries Proteus and Silvia marries Valentine.

Discussion: A slight play and one which is largely a comedy of words rather than of situations or actions, but one which is as elegant as an Astaire and Rogers dance number. The pacing is meticulous and the speeches show Shakespeare at his best. The depth is provided by the theme of the conflict between love and friendship.

Background: The play is drawn from the surrounds of the playwright, London in the sixteenth century and the characters are reflections of those around him.

Films: Far too serious a production from the BBC in 1983. Faithful to the lines, but not to the spirit.

Verdict: Light, entertaining and witty, rather than bawdy, it is a perfectly executed five-finger exercise. 4/5

The Taming Of The Shrew (1592)

There 's small choice in rotten apples.

(Act i. Sc. 1.)

Story: This is a play within a play. The framing play is that of an attempt to convince Christopher Sly, a drunkard, that he is actually a lord who fell asleep for fifteen years. The play within the play is that of the star-crossed love between Katherine, the shrew of the title, and Petruchio, a roistering and impoverished noble from Verona, who has come to find a rich wife in Padua.

Petruchio encounters Katherine through Hortensio, a friend of his who is one of the suitors to Bianca, Katherine's younger sister. Their father, Baptista, will not allow Bianca to marry before Katherine, and Katherine drives away all her suitors. When Petruchio is assured of a generous dowry, he takes on the challenge. After engaging in a battle of wits with Katherine, Petruchio informs Baptista that he's mightily pleased with her and they arrange a marriage.

Petruchio turns up for the wedding in clothes which are tatterdemalion and deliberately chosen to irritate Katherine. He brawls and disrupts the wedding, and then drags Katherine off to his run-down estate without staying for the wedding feast. This is where the real confrontation takes place with Petruchio gradually wearing down Katherine's resistance and, oddly, gaining her love. Then they return to Padua, to settle a bet Petruchio has made.

Lucentio, another suitor, has beaten Hortensio for Bianca's hand and secretly married her, but Hortensio is not too upset. Petruchio wins his bet by proving that Katherine has become gentle, and all exit happily.

Discussion: While, perhaps, not totally in tune with modern sensibilities, *The Taming Of The Shrew* is bawdy, rollicking and full of good humour and irony. It takes two strong characters and surrounds them with a marvellous supporting cast while they fight each other hammer and tongs. There is a joyous wordplay and everyone has a part in the fun.

The play is quite short, as is necessary for what is a fairly slight plot, and the pace never lets up. The acts of the core play are very short—act II has only one scene—so the audience is swept away by the sheer merriment and never has a chance to be critical.

Background: The play is drawn from an earlier one by Marlowe. There are also elements of Gascoine's *Supposes* and a hint of Ariosto but it would only be necessary for Shakespeare to look out his window into the rowdy Elizabethan streets to find the characters.

Films: The film which gets closest to the spirit of the play is undoubtedly the Elizabeth Taylor/Richard Burton version with its hugely physical rendition. Petruchio literally knocks down walls in his pursuit of Kate. Mention should also be given to an episode of *Moonlighting* which pursues the plot of the play, without ever quite catching it, with vast élan and good humour. The image of the horse wearing Ray-Bans is unforgettable.

Verdict: Few plays give as much scope to the actors to have a good time and carry the audience along with them. When well-produced, it is riotously funny. 5/5

Richard The Third (1592)

I have set my life upon a cast,
and I will stand the hazard of the die.

(Act v. Sc. 4.)

Story: The play begins with Richard warning us of his evil intent, which he then implements by courting Anne, the wife of Edward (who he has had murdered), during the funeral procession of Henry VI (who he murdered himself). Richard then sows dissent at the court of King Edward IV and arranges to have Edward's brother, Clarence, murdered. He convinces Edward that this was his fault and Edward dies of an illness, perhaps aided by his feelings of guilt.

Edward's son, Edward V, is next in line for the throne but Richard usurps it before he can be crowned on the grounds that Edward is illegitimate. He kills Hastings, Edward's main supporter, and sends Edward and his brother to the Tower of London. Richard continues to kill off people who threaten him, including the two Princes in the Tower.

Richard's actions alienate Anne and Buckingham, one of his erstwhile supporters. The Earl of Richmond brings rebel armies against Richard and Buckingham leads one of these. Buckingham is captured and Richard orders him to be brought to Salisbury, where he intends to battle Richmond. He executes Buckingham and prepares for the deciding battle.

Ghosts visit Richard in his tent and warn him of the coming defeat. He fights bravely the next day but the prophecy comes true; his forces are defeated and he is killed by Richmond. Richmond takes the crown and becomes King Henry VII. He swears that he will end the wars in England and marries Elizabeth, Edward IV's widow, to accomplish this.

Discussion: Richard strides through this play as a villain of heroic proportions. It almost seems unjust that he is defeated at the end because he is such a truly splendid villain. He plots, connives, murders and betrays throughout the play with remarkable gusto, hypocritical to the end. Those who oppose him seem quite lacklustre by comparison.

Again, Shakespeare seems to give the best speeches to his villains, and Richard's are superb, sufficiently convincing to seduce a widow at her husband's funeral. He manipulates people with his words and only when he has achieved his ambition, when he actually has the power he craved, do things fall apart. Perhaps he simply killed too many people. There are, after all, eleven ghosts which visit him in his tent before Bosworth Field. It's difficult to trust a man like that.

Background: The story is probably drawn from Holinshed but mainly from Sir Thomas More's account of the rise and fall of Richard.

Films: The Richard Loncraine adaptation of the play, from 1995, is superb, beautifully filmed and acted, even though it sets the play in 1930s England. The more faithful 1983 BBC production is utterly different in style but just about as good.

Verdict: The grandest of villainy, with one of the most eloquent of villains, abounding with action, a marvellous play. 5/5

Love's Labour's Lost (1593)

> For where is any author in the world teaches such beauty as a
> woman's eye?

> (Act iv. Sc. 3.)

Story: Ferdinand, King of Navarre, has set up an institute of higher
learning wherein all must sign articles, lasting for three years, that they
will not speak to a woman, nor fall in love. These rules are immediately
challenged by the arrival of a delegation from France, headed by the
Princess. The problem is solved by meeting the delegation a mile outside the academy, where the rules do not apply.

Ferdinand falls in love with the Princess, and other signatories to the
articles, Armand, Longaville, Dumain and Biron, fall in love, as well;
Armand with a peasant girl, Jacquenetta, and the others with the Princess' three ladies-in-waiting, Rosaline, Maria and Katherine. A series of
letters from various lovers to their ladies, misplaced and overheard, sets
the scene for the final dilemma. All the men are in love but they need a
means to break their vows without penalty and with some honour pre-
served. Biron, the most quick-witted of the group, argues that love is
more important than vows, and they all band together to pursue their
loves.

Their pursuit is successful but on a condition. They must all pursue
good works for twelve months and a day to prove their love. All the lovers accept this condition, heartened by the fact that Armand must work
on a farm for three years to win Jacquenetta.

Discussion: As light as swans down, and as warm. There is not a beat
missed in the entire play. It is beautifully constructed, witty and charming. The dominant characters are Biron and Rosaline but all the characters are well drawn. The basis of the play is love and how impossible it
is for lusty young men to avoid it. The project Ferdinand sets up with
his academy is doomed from the start. Biron knows it, and so does the
audience.

The dialogue lacks the bawdy belly laughs of plays such as *The Taming Of The Shrew*, but more than makes up for that in elegance and wit. It is a more intellectual play than most of the comedies, not in its subject matter, but in the sharpness of the encounters between the characters. Biron's long speeches, wherein he develops witty arguments for whatever suits his purpose at the time, are masterpieces.

Background: The play was probably written to be performed privately. It is an invention of Shakespeare's, drawn from his own imagination and the events of the times, much like a modern revue.

Films: Despite a good cast, the 1985 BBC production is a little slow, but it seems to be the only game in town.

Verdict: Heartwarming farce, filled with humour and hope. 5/5

Romeo And Juliet (1593)

It seems she hangs upon the cheek of night like a rich jewel
in an Ethiope's ear.

(Act i. Sc. 5.)

Story: The Montagues and Capulets, two families in Verona, are bitter enemies. Escalus, the Prince of Verona, has warned them that there
will be severe penalties for any further fighting between their factions.
The scene for disaster is set when Romeo of the Montagues fall in love
with Juliet of the Capulets. He woos her and wins her, and secretly marries her, with the help of Friar Laurence.

The day after their wedding night, Tybalt, a Capulet, kills Romeo's
best friend, Mercutio. Inflamed with revenge, Romeo kills Tybalt.
When he realises what he has done, he flees Verona, hoping that he can
return when things have cooled down. In the meantime, Juliet's parents,
unaware of her marriage, have promised her to another nobleman, the
County Paris. To avoid this, Juliet obtains a potion from Friar Laurence
which will give her the appearance of death for forty-two hours. In this
time, Laurence will send a message to Romeo, who can return and
secretly carry her away.

Juliet takes the potion and is placed in her tomb but the message to
Romeo goes astray and he hears from another that she's dead. He
returns to Verona, enters the tomb and takes poison by Juliet's bier.
Moments later, Laurence arrives and discovers the body, then Juliet
wakes up. She sees Romeo and Laurence tries to get her to leave with
him, but she stays and, after Laurence leaves to avoid the approaching
watchmen, she kills herself next to Romeo's body. The Watch takes the
bodies to Escalus, who points out this tragedy to the families.

Discussion: In both characters and language, this play captures the
essence of romance and youth. The passion which leads Romeo and
Juliet to their marriage also leads them to their deaths, since it can allow
no compromise. It is, equally, passion which leads Romeo to kill Tybalt
after Mercutio's death. In both cases, it is passion out of control, with-

out the tempering wisdom of age and experience. This, however, is its attraction, this wild passion of youth.

There are some faults with the play but these are overshadowed by the language, which touches the heart more than any other of Shakespeare's plays. This is just as well, since the appeal to the intellect is not great. It is not a subtle, nor a particularly complex play, in the fashion of *Hamlet* or *The Tempest*, but rather one which sweeps the audience up in the high drama of the affair between its two star-crossed lovers.

Background: The story is derived from *The Tragical History Of Romeus and Juliet*, a poem by Arthur Brooke, and was also available as prose in *The Palace Of Pleasure* by Painter. Shakespeare has added the character of Mercutio and sped up events so that the play takes place over a span of five days.

Films: While there have been attempts to modernise the play, as in the 1996 Baz Lurman production *Romeo+Juliet*, and derivations of it, as in 1961's *West Side Story*, the defining version is the Franco Zeffirelli film of 1968, with its opulent set and stunning performances, particularly from Michael York, John McEnery and Olivia Hussey.

Verdict: Everything in the play depends on the audience believing that young teenagers can speak as poetically as these do. The language is beautiful but the plot is doubtful. 4/5

A Midsummer Night's Dream (1594)

The course of true love never did run smooth.

(Act i. Sc. 1.)

Story: There are three stories within the play, all occurring within the framing story of the wedding of Duke Theseus to Hippolyta in Athens. The lovers Hermia and Lysander flee to the forest to avoid Hermia's forced marriage to Demetrius. Helena, Hermia's friend who loves Demetrius, tells him of this and they follow, Helena hoping to win his love in the process. In the forest, there's dissension between Oberon and Titania, the King and Queen of the fairies, over a changeling child they both desire as their henchman. To resolve this and gain revenge on Titania, Oberon employs his servant Puck to gain a flower whose juice, laid on sleeping eyes, causes the recipient to fall in love with the next creature they see. He intends to cause Titania to fall in love with something vile and then take the child.

Puck gains the flower but Oberon has heard the lovers and instructs Puck to anoint their eyes to make sure that each lover winds up with the right woman. Also in the forest is a group of artisans, practising a play for the duke's wedding, led by Nick Bottom, the weaver. Puck places an ass' head on Bottom then anoints Titania's eyes. She wakes and falls in love with him. Puck has also anointed the eyes of the lovers but has mistaken them so that confusion reigns.

After many mistakes and much comedy, all errors are corrected and the lovers return to Athens to reconcile with Hermia's father. The artisans put on their play, *Pyramus And Thisbe*, and are rewarded for their comic performance of this tragedy. Oberon and Titania bless the wedding and the house and all ends happily.

Discussion: The play is not deep, although there are references within it to the politics of the times, but it has excellent characterisation: Oberon, in particular, is a character of great depth; Puck and Bottom are superb comic creations. The play works on our emotions rather than our intellects, with its themes of marriage, love crossed, recrossed and reconciled. It is the joyous model of love of which *Romeo And Juliet* is the sombre shadow. Puck has the defining line, perhaps for both plays, when he says to Oberon, "Lord, what fools these mortals be."

Background: The play was written for a wedding, most probably that of Sir Thomas Heneage and the Countess of Southampton, in 1593. There are several sources, primarily Chaucer's *The Knight's Tale*. Ovid provides the basis for the *Pyramus And Thisbe* play, and Spenser's poem *The Faerie Queene* provides Oberon, but much of the play comes from folk tales and myths, largely drawn, as are the artisans, from Shakespeare's own Warwickshire.

Films: The best version remains that of 1935, directed by Max Reinhardt and William Dieterle, with its superb Mendelssohn music and stunning cinematography, for which Hal Mohr won the Oscar. The 1999 version, with Calista Flockhart, Kevin Kline and Michelle Pfeiffer, is also a good one.

Verdict: You go home from the play feeling satisfied with the world. One of Shakespeare's best. 5/5.

Richard The Second (1595)

For God's sake, let us sit upon the ground and tell sad stories
of the death of kings.

(Act iii. Sc. 2.)

Story The play opens with Lord Bolingbroke bringing a case of treason before Richard, a case against Lord Mowbray. The two are prepared
to fight over this but Richard won't allow it and exiles them both, Mowbray for life, but Bolingbroke for only six years, thanks to an appeal by
his father, John of Gaunt. They both go into exile.

Richard has war in Ireland and cannot find the funds for his armies.
An opportunity arises when John of Gaunt dies, and Richard seizes all
his estates. Bolingbroke discovers this and gathers an army to take back
his inheritance. While Richard is in Ireland, Bolingbroke gains the support of the Duke of York, who has been left in charge of the country. By
the time Richard returns, the Lords and Commons have largely sided
with Bolingbroke, who makes Richard into his virtual prisoner when he
catches him at Flint castle. They return to London. At Westminster,
Bolingbroke discovers more of the plots and murders which occurred
during Richard's reign. Richard reluctantly yields the crown to him and
is sent to the Tower of London. Bolingbroke takes the throne as Henry
IV.

Almost immediately, there is a plot to overthrow the new king. York
discovers it and warns Bolingbroke, even though his own son is impli-
cated. The king spares York's son, upon the plea of his mother, but condemns the rest of the conspirators. In his passion, he makes a rash
remark; two lords take it literally, and kill Richard. The king is appalled
by this, exiles the killers and pledges to make a pilgrimage to the Holy
Land to atone.

Discussion: Richard II is marked by the amazing poetry of the dialogue. Richard, in particular, has lines of great power and elegance. The
plum speech, though, belongs to John of Gaunt on his deathbed, when
he defines England and all that it is. It is the dialogue which transforms

a fairly straightforward play of political skulduggery in the palace into something quite remarkable.

The play also sets the scene for the turmoil which follows in *Henry IV, V & VI*. The way in which Bolingbroke becomes King Henry IV, the death of Richard and the political mess he leaves behind him are all key factors in the War of the Roses which follows. Even by the end of this play, the fragile allegiances show signs of wear. The reign of Henry IV begins in blood, despite his attempts to avoid this.

Background: Again, the story is mainly drawn from Holinshed, although there were many accounts of the death of Richard. Shakespeare also drew upon *Thomas Of Woodstock*, an anonymous play.

Films: This is one of the BBC's finest productions. The 1978 version has a magnificent cast, with Derek Jacobi, John Gielgud, John Finch and Wendy Hiller, and they wring the best from the play.

Verdict: The language is gorgeous and the characters of Richard, Bolingbroke and Gaunt are beautifully crafted. The portrait of the weak, gullible Richard is superb, and his whining and carping at the end of his power is still magnificent. 4/5

The Merchant Of Venice (1596)

> The villainy you teach me I will execute, and it shall go hard,
> but I will better the instruction.

(Act iii. Sc. 1.)

Story: Antonio is a merchant of Venice and has difficulties because his ships have not arrived back. He goes surety for his friend, Bassanio, to borrow money from Shylock, a Jewish moneylender. Bassanio needs the money to court a rich heiress, Portia. Because of Antonio's previous persecution of him and his arrogant manner, Shylock extorts a contract from Antonio for a pound of his flesh if he does not make good the debt by the due date.

Shylock's daughter, Jessica, has fallen in love with Lorenzo, a Christian, and leaves with him as Bassanio is leaving to woo Portia. She takes her jewels with her and this enrages Shylock against Christians even more. He discovers that Antonio's ships have sunk but this does not mollify him.

Bassanio wins the hand of Portia, but Lorenzo and Jessica arrive with the news that Shylock intends to cut out Antonio's heart. Bassanio rushes to aid him, backed with Portia's money. Portia follows soon after, with Jessica and Nerissa, her maidservant, who has fallen in love with Gratiano, another friend of Bassanio.

Shylock is ready to take his pound of flesh, despite all the pleas and offers to make good of Bassanio and others, when Portia arrives, disguised as a male lawyer. She cannot overturn the contract but argues that it must be followed to the letter; exactly a pound, no blood. Shylock realises he can't do this and tries to fall back on the other offers but is held to have defaulted on the contract so he is punished by having his property taken from him and is forced to become Christian.

With a few gentle tricks between the lovers to assure their love, the play ends.

Discussion: The destruction of Shylock makes it difficult for a modern audience to understand that this is a comedy. Sensibilities were different in the sixteenth century, where Shylock, with his exaggerated characteristics, was considered a figure of fun. Even with this in mind, Shylock is a very thought-provoking figure, particularly when he lists the injuries he has suffered from Christians and the reasons for his desire for revenge.

Portia's argument regarding the contract and the pound of flesh is, of course, nonsense and would never stand up in a real court, but it gives the court an excuse to save Antonio and penalise Shylock. Her emphasis on the fact that the State would gain by this may well be one of the factors affecting the duke's judgement.

The romance between the lovers is fun and full of lovers' games, except for that between Lorenzo and Jessica, which is a little more serious. The fifth act is very short, only a single scene, and is quite different in language and style from the rest of the play. It seems almost tacked on to resolve the comic aspects of the lovers' affairs.

Background: The play draws heavily on Marlowe's *The Jew Of Malta*, with constant topical references added in. Shakespeare moves the events to Venice, perhaps influenced by another Italian story on the same theme.

Films: The Victorian setting of the 1973 Jonathan Miller production works very well, and Laurence Olivier is a good Shylock, but even Lord Larry is shaded by the rich performance of Warren Mitchell in the BBC's 1980 production.

Verdict: Like the curates egg, parts are excellent. The fifth act, while quite gorgeous, seems somehow unnecessary. 4/5

King John (1596)

For he is but a bastard to the time that doth not smack of observation.

(Act i. Sc. 1.)

Story: King John goes to France to reclaim the English possessions there but a disagreement over John's nephew, Arthur, and France's claims to England and Ireland lead to war. The war is stalemated before the gates of Angier, when a compromise is reached. If John's niece, Blanch, marries Lewis, son of Philip, the King of France, then the war is over. Despite violent protests by Arthur's mother, Constance, the deal is done.

Unfortunately, there is trouble before the wedding, stirred up by Constance and the Bastard, an illegitimate son of Richard I and John's nephew. The wedding takes place but the peace is shattered. John seizes Arthur and places him in the care of Lord Hubert de Burgh. John defeats the French, with the aid of the Bastard, and sends a message to Hubert to kill Arthur. Hubert can't do it but tells Richard that he has.

The victory is short-lived and the French invade England. On top of this, the people have heard of Arthur's death and are on the verge of rebellion. Hubert tells John that Arthur is alive and rushes to produce him for the lords, telling them the news first. Arthur, however, attempts to escape confinement and falls to his death. The lords join the French.

In the war, fortunes ebb and flow and, even though John has given up his crown, peace cannot be achieved until John dies. His son, Henry, ascends the throne and accepts a brokered, but uneasy, peace.

Discussion: A straightforward story. The characters are well drawn and there are some beautiful scenes, such as the bitch fight between Constance and Elinor, and Arthur's appeal to Hubert. The Bastard is a muscular creation and his insouciant, relentless taunting of Austria before they fight is great comedy.

Background: There was an anonymous play around at the time called *The Troublesome Reign Of John, King Of England*. That, along with Holinshed, almost certainly formed the basis of this play.

Films: Claire Bloom is Constance in the 1984 BBC production and does a very good job. On the whole, the production is very worthwhile, breathing life into a somewhat neglected play.

Verdict: Direct, craftsmanlike and entertaining, this is a bread-and-butter play, satisfying without being fancy. 4/5

Henry IV, Part One (1597)

There live not three good men unhanged in England;
and one of them is fat and grows old.

(Act ii. Sc. 4.)

Story: The country is wracked by war and Henry has the doubtful support of the Earl of Northumberland, Hotspur (his son) and the Earl of Worcester. Henry's son, Prince Hal, is roistering with some ill-chosen companions instead of fighting at his father's side. At a conference, Henry angers Hotspur, who vows to bring down the king and the prince. Hotspur, Northumberland and Worcester plot to achieve this and to put Mortimer, Earl of March, on the throne.

While this plot is being hatched, Hal and his companions, including Sir John Falstaff, are enjoying life until a messenger arrives summoning them to battle. When Hal and Henry meet, Henry chides his son for his wastrel behaviour and Hal decides to win his father's approval by killing Hotspur. They prepare for war and Hal buys Falstaff a company of foot soldiers.

Despite all efforts to achieve peace, battle is joined. In the battle, Hal saves Henry's life and then kills Hotspur. Falstaff, who has been playing dead nearby, bloodies his sword in the body after Hal leaves and takes credit for the kill. The king wins the day, Hal is restored to favour and Falstaff is ready for a reward. The execution of a couple of Yorkist lords brings a temporary peace.

Discussion: A splendid play, which overcomes the stuffiness of the king by the marvellous vitality of Prince Hal. Falstaff is a magnificent invention and serves to connect Hal with the real world of brawling, bawdy liars and thieves. This is good training for the throne given the state of the aristocracy at the time. Hal, too, is a wonderful character, able to relate to the basest as well as the most noble. The trilogy of the two-part *Henry IV* and *Henry V* is the greatest of Shakespeare's histories, showing the full power of a writer at the height of his abilities with a subject worthy of his mettle.

Background: Drawn from Holinshed, but Shakespeare may also have drawn on an anonymous play, *The Famous Victories Of Henry The Fifth*. There are, of course, alterations to history for dramatic purpose; Hotspur was twenty-three years older than Prince Hal, who was only sixteen. Henry IV was only thirty-seven, and in the prime of life, rather than as aged and worn as the play portrays him.

Films: Chimes At Midnight (aka *Falstaff*) was Orson Welles' superb 1965 adaptation and amalgamation of the trilogy. As a representation of the plays, it is a work of genius. A more faithful version is the 1979 BBC production, but it lacks exuberance.

Verdict: It is really necessary to read, or see, *Richard II* through to *Henry V* to get the full impact of these history plays, but this one serves to introduce Prince Hal and Falstaff, two of Shakespeare's best-realised characters, who reappear in later plays. 5/5

Henry IV, Part Two (1598)

We have heard the chimes at midnight.

(Act iii. Sc. 2.)

Story: Henry has won the previous battle but war is still at hand. The Earl of Northumberland has decided to take the field against Henry to avenge the death of his son, Hotspur, and Scroop, the Bishop of York, is coming to aid him. The French and the Welsh also threaten Henry, which gives the rebels an added advantage. They go to war but Northumberland is persuaded by Hotspur's widow not to join them—he goes to Scotland and is ready to return if the rebels prevail.

Jack Falstaff, Prince Hal's boon companion, also prepares for war in his own way by avoiding the debts he owes and paying his last respects to his old drinking companions. He shares a few tender moments with Doll Tearsheet, a tart and an old friend, before he is summoned to war along with his prince.

Henry does not want war and mourns the deaths of the rebels who were once his friends. His woes are increased when Lord Westmoreland, the leader of his forces, tricks the rebels into dispersing and then kills their leaders. Henry is ill and this news does not help him. Hal rushes back to his father's side and they are finally reconciled just before Henry dies. Hal takes the throne and convinces the lords that his wastrel ways are behind him now. As token of this, in one of the most poignant scenes in the play, he rejects Falstaff and banishes him. No gesture could more convince the nobles of Hal's reform.

Discussion: Although the title is *Henry IV*, the play belongs to Falstaff. In the face of his vast vitality, the battles and betrayals of the lords of the land somehow become pale and petty, squabbles of children who have yet to learn how to live. Even Hal is lessened in our eyes when he becomes an echo of the upright, moral Henry. There is, somehow, a hollowness in Henry, an insincerity which causes him to turn a blind eye to the dishonesty of his lieutenants when they betray the rebel leaders. Prior to assuming the crown, Hal has never been this way. Instead, he has been honest-hearted and kind. The kindness lingers when, even as he rejects him, he grants Falstaff a pardon. But he is not what he was.

Part of the reason for this lies in his realisation, as he watched over the dying king, of the weight of the crown, of what it means to be the ruler of a troubled nation. He knows that he must unite the country and vows to pass the crown on to his heirs. But to do this he needs the support of the nobles and the people, and their respect. His father, after all, usurped the throne. He can't get respect as the Jack the Lad he used to be. Thus, he must forget his old life, and begin anew. Falstaff can have no part in his new life.

But the triumph remains with Falstaff. Spurned, banished and warned to change his ways, he is unbowed and his last act in the play is to take Shallow, his old drinking companion, off to dinner, assuring him that the king will call for him soon, which is when Shallow will get the thousand pounds Falstaff owes him.

Background: As for *Henry IV, Part One.*

Films: Welles' *Chimes At Midnight* again, and the 1979 BBC version, although this is not as good as their production of the first part of the play.

Verdict: Without Falstaff the play would be good, but not entertaining, full of serious doings of lords and kings. With him, it provides a peculiar insight into the hearts of men. 4/5

As You Like It (1598)

All the world 's a stage,
and all the men and women merely players.

(Act ii. Sc. 7.)

Story: Duke Frederick has usurped the ducal throne and banished the rightful duke to the Forest of Arden. To make amends his daughter Celia has made Rosalind, the duke's daughter, heir to the estate. In the meantime, Oliver, the older son of Sir Rowland de Boys, has arranged to have his younger brother Orlando killed in a wrestling bout in front of Frederick.

Orlando wins the bout and also the heart of Rosalind but has to leave quickly, with no reward, to avoid the wrath of Frederick, who was his father's enemy. Frederick banishes Rosalind, who dresses as a man and goes to the forest to find her father. Celia follows her and Orlando also heads for the forest, warned that he will be killed if he returns home. Orlando is taken in by the duke and his men, including the melancholy Jacques. Frederick confiscates all Oliver's property until he finds and brings back Orlando to face punishment, so Oliver also heads for the forest.

Rosalind, disguised as a man, tricks Orlando into following her instructions on how to be a lover and there are mistaken identities galore as people fall in love with one another, with very comic results. Oliver eventually arrives, tells how Orlando saved him from a lion and says that he has changed because of this. He gives up the estate to Orlando, willing to become a shepherd in the forest with Celia, with whom he's fallen in love. Rosalind predicts that all the confusion will be sorted out and everyone happily married. She's correct and all the lovers receive the news that Frederick, too, has had a change of heart— he has gone to live with a monk, giving up the material world and returning all the estates the rightful duke. Jacques decides to join him and the play ends.

Discussion: The mistaken identities and disguises could have made this a simple farce but they don't because of Rosalind. Her wit and wisdom supply the perfect counterfoil to Orlando's blundering courtship, and their love affair provides the core around which the rest of the plot revolves. The trickery she uses to gull him into revealing his heart is gentle and witty, rather than acerbic. This is possibly because Orlando is no match for her, whereas in plays such as *Much Ado About Nothing*, Benedick and Beatrice are well matched. Far more than in most of Shakespeare's plays, the lead character is female.

The plot is, of course, highly improbable but that's to be expected in a comedy. The sudden changes of heart of Oliver and Frederick and the unexpected arrival of Hymen are only incidental to the main story. The main theme is simply a celebration of love. Even the sinister characters are only bad for a while. Jacques, while melancholy, is almost triumphantly so, determined to resist all this happiness around him. And even if the plot is full of improbabilities, who cares? The action is fast, the dialogue is witty and everybody is happy at the end.

Background: Derived from *Rosalynde, Euphues' Golden Legacy* by Thomas Lodge, the play contains more than a few references to Marlowe, whose *Hero And Leander* was published in the same year, posthumously.

Films: The delightful Helen Mirren stars in the 1978 BBC version of this play, and makes a meal of the part of Rosalind, although the staging is a little stiff.

Verdict: A bright, witty comedy for the sake of sheer entertainment, with the gloomy Jacques to give it a little depth. 5/5

Julius Caesar (1599)

There is a tide in the affairs of men which taken at the flood,
leads on to fortune.

(Act iv. Sc. 3.)

Story: Julius Caesar has been offered the kingship of Rome and, even
though he has refused it, there are fears he will accept it if offered again.
A group of senators, led by Cassius, Marcellus and Casca, conspire to
prevent this by murdering Caesar. As part of their conspiracy they
attempt to get Brutus, a very influential senator from an old family, to
join them. Initially, he refuses, but they convince him that it is for the
good of Rome, and so reluctantly he joins them.

Their plan is to kill Caesar on the ides of March, the 15th, in the
Forum but Caesar has had omens that this is not a good day and nearly
stays home. Decius Brutus, another conspirator, convinces him to go
and Caesar attends with Marc Antony, his best friend and henchman.
Caesar is stabbed to death by the conspirators in the senate but they
leave Marc Antony alive. Later, Brutus assures him of his safety and
allows him to speak after him to the public, to explain Caesar's death.
Brutus speaks to them first, with reasoned arguments, but Antony
inflames their passions and incites them to revenge Caesar's death.

Civil war follows with Antony on one side and Brutus and the conspirators on the other. They meet on the plains of Philippi, and the conspirators are on the verge of winning when Antony breaks through and
reverses the course of the battle. Cassius and Brutus both commit suicide to avoid being returned to Rome as captives.

Discussion: It is difficult to decide which character suffers the
greater tragedy, Caesar or Brutus. Caesar's downfall comes about
through his susceptibility to flattery; Brutus' comes about through his
excessive nobility. Caesar falls through not knowing himself, while
Brutus falls through not understanding others.

It is the character of Marc Antony who shines through, though. Cunning, smart and unscrupulous, he is a far fitter match for Cassius and the

conspirators than either Caesar or Brutus. He understands the political necessities which surround him and he responds to them to both save his own skin and avenge Caesar.

The play is about politics and envy, and how these can bring about the downfall of even the greatest, while lesser men survive. As Antony says of Brutus at the end:

> "all the conspirators save only he
> Did what they did in envy of great Caesar;
> He only, in a general honest thought
> And common good to all, made one of them."

Background: The source for this play is undoubtedly Plutarch and most probably the translation by Sir Thomas North.

Films: There have been many versions of *Julius Caesar*, but the most attractive is probably the 1953 version, directed by Joseph Mankiewicz and starring the young Marlon Brando as Marc Antony.

Verdict: The play is one of Shakespeare's shorter works and moves quickly. The set piece speeches are marvellous and the characters beautifully realised. The last two acts, wherein the battle takes place, seem less well constructed. 4/5

Much Ado About Nothing (1599)

He that hath a beard is more than a youth,
and he that hath no beard is less than a man.

(Act ii. Sc. 1.)

Story: Don Pedro, the Prince of Aragon, his brother Don John, Claudio and Benedick have all returned to Messina from war. While Benedick laments the passing of the true bachelor, Claudio falls in love with Hero, the daughter of Leonato, a lord of Messina. Don Pedro supports Claudio and achieves their betrothal, then plots to match Benedick with Beatrice, Leonato's niece.

Don John, out of sheer malice, conspires to prevent Claudio's marriage and succeeds in this with the help of Borachio, one of his henchmen. However, the Watch apprehends Borachio, but not in time to prevent the wedding being disrupted. Claudio rejects Hero—she faints and they believe her dead. Benedick suspects Don John and, when Hero recovers, hatches a plot with Beatrice to discover the truth. They pretend to bury Hero.

Dogberry of the Watch has extracted the story from Borachio, and Don John has run off. Dogberry brings Borachio before Leonato, Don Pedro and Claudio, and Borachio confesses in time to stop a series of duels being fought over the events of the wedding. However, Don Pedro and Claudio must make amends by singing at Hero's tomb and repeating this every year. They sing at the tomb and Claudio promises to marry the woman of Leonato's choice, which proves to be the resurrected Hero. The situation is explained and Beatrice and Benedick go off to be married as news is brought of Don John's apprehension.

Discussion: The play contains a more finely-tuned version of the battle of the sexes from *The Taming Of The Shrew*. The dialogue between Beatrice and Benedick is some of Shakespeare's wittiest, and their love scene is in some ways more touching than anything in *Romeo And Juliet*. Their love for each other, when they finally admit it exists, is the love of adults rather than the simple passion of children, and they come to it by a hard road of argument and insult, as do Kate and Petruchio.

The plot is a complex one because of all the skulduggery. Don John seems a peculiarly ineffectual Shakespearean villain because his plans come to naught. No one suffers any permanent harm from them. The plans of the others do bear fruit, in marriages and reconciliations, which perhaps goes to show that true love will always triumph and evil will always be punished.

Background: There would seem to be no single source for the play, but elements of many, including *Orlando Furioso* and Spenser's *The Faerie Queene*. But Shakespeare stirred the pot and added in sub-plots and new characters, echoing the life of London all around him.

Films: Kenneth Branagh adapted this play in 1993 and did it well. The entire cast, with the exception of Keanu Reeves as Don John, turn in fine performances, and the joy of the play is very obvious in the film.

Verdict: A superb comedy, by a writer at the height of his powers. 5/5

Henry V (1599)

We few, we happy few, we band of brothers.

(Act iv. Sc. 3.)

Story: Henry wants to re-establish his rule over French territories and, after provocation from the French, decides to take an army to France. But first he executes three lords who have been hired by the French to kill him, then he sails for France with his army.

Henry sends Lord Exeter to demand the crown but the French King refuses and offers, instead, his daughter, Katherine, and some minor provinces. Henry rejects this and lays siege to and conquers Harfleur, an important French town. He continues his triumphs all the way to Champagne, then leads his men to Calais, where he intends to winter. The French King sends a threat to Henry, who wishes to avoid battle, but will not run away from it. The forces will meet at Agincourt.

They fight on St Crispian's day and, despite being outnumbered five to one, Henry is victorious. More than that; they have destroyed ten thousand enemy, for the loss of twenty-eight of their own. After the battle, Henry meets with the French court to determine the terms of their submission and he woos and wins Katherine, the Princess. This intended marriage allows the French King to agree to all the conditions, including naming Henry as the heir to the French throne. For the moment, all are satisfied.

Discussion: The play moves quickly, even with the interpolated comic scenes with Pistol and others. These scenes from the life of the lesser classes serve to balance out the scenes with the nobles and lend a depth to the play which might not exist without them. The death of Falstaff and the role of Pistol, one of his old companions, serve to link this play with the two parts of *Henry IV*. With Falstaff's death, the roistering youth of Henry also seems to disappear and we are shown not only the warrior of the previous plays but the statesman he has become. He is ruthless when it is necessary, as when he deals with the three traitors and at Agincourt when he orders the prisoner killed, but merciful when he can be. He has become someone who can make hard decisions without regret.

The aftermath affects the audience more than the battle of Agincourt. The enormous loss of French life, compared to that of the English, and the list of French nobles who fell has a powerful impact. While the French are shown as, perhaps, a little vapid and very arrogant, they are also merry and vital. With the resolution achieved after the battle, these deaths seem so unnecessary.

Background: Holinshed was, again, the main source for the events of the play but Shakespeare also followed the anonymous play *The Famous Victories Of Henry The Fifth*, which was available to him.

Films: Even though they are vastly different in style, there is little to choose between the 1944 Laurence Olivier version and the 1989 Kenneth Branagh version. They are both superb.

Verdict: So much happens, and the comedy is beautifully contrasted with some of Shakespeare's most powerful martial speeches. 5/5

Hamlet (1600)

To be honest as this world goes,
is to be one man picked out of ten thousand.

(Act ii. Sc. 2.)

Story: Prince Hamlet's father, Hamlet, dies and when Hamlet returns
from Wittenberg University to Denmark for the burial, he finds that his
uncle, Claudius, has married his mother, Gertrude. He then discovers,
from his father's ghost, that Claudius murdered him. He swears revenge
and pretends to be mad to cover his intent.

At first Polonius, Claudius' adviser, believes that the madness is
caused by Hamlet's love for his daughter Ophelia but when this is
tested, Hamlet rejects Ophelia and sends her away. Claudius brings in
two old friends of Hamlet's, Rosencrantz and Guildenstern, to spy on
him but Hamlet evades their questioning. Hamlet then employs a group
of strolling players to test the king with a play similar in circumstance to
old Hamlet's death. Claudius reacts in a way which proves him guilty
and Hamlet has an opportunity to kill him, but refrains. He is summoned to speak with his mother and berates her for her marriage to
Claudius. He kills the hidden Polonius, believing him to be the king.
Claudius responds by banishing Hamlet to England accompanied by
Rosencrantz and Guildenstern, who carry letters instructing the English
King to kill Hamlet.

Hamlet is rescued and returned to Denmark but he has replaced the
letters carried by Rosencrantz and Guildenstern with ones requiring
their deaths. He arrives back to see Ophelia's burial. While he was away
she went mad and committed suicide. Her brother, Laertes, blames both
her death and that of Polonius on Hamlet and conspires with Claudius to
kill him.

Claudius proposes a friendly duel, but Laertes' sword will be sharp
and poisoned and Claudius will offer Hamlet poisoned wine. Hamlet
accepts the challenge but things go wrong. Hamlet refuses the wine.
Gertrude drinks it. Then, after Laertes wounds Hamlet with the poi-

soned sword, they exchange swords and Hamlet wounds Laertes. Dying, Laertes reveals the plot and asks for forgiveness. Gertrude dies and Hamlet kills Claudius before his own death. His last act is to ask his best friend, Horatio, to tell the world the truth of the events.

Discussion: Hamlet is undoubtedly the play most associated with Shakespeare. It is also the most popular of Shakespeare's plays. The central figure of the moody, uncertain Prince of Denmark is both strikingly modern and, simultaneously, classic. His uncertainty forms one of the major themes of the play. He is driven to revenge, yet he does not take it when opportunity offers.

Hamlet sums up his feelings in his soliloquy, wondering whether it is better to suffer in silence, or to fight and die. He discusses death as a release from the struggles of the world, one which he seeks, but is too cowardly to take, since he knows not what comes after death. It is, perhaps, this reflection on death and why people go on living when life itself seems intolerable which makes the play fascinating to audiences and academics alike.

Combined with this philosophy is a rousing story of the supernatural, treachery, murder, madness and revenge. The body count in *Hamlet* is one of the highest in his tragedies, and the play combines both some of Shakespeare's deepest tragedy, and some of his best comedy. Polonius is a perfect comic foil for Hamlet, which makes his death all the more tragic, and the scene with the grave-digger is wit at its highest.

Background: The story is an old one, drawn from *Saxo Grammaticus* and Belleforest's *Histoires Tragiques*.

Films: Almost every year produces a new interpretation of *Hamlet* on film. It has been filmed in almost every language in which films are made. The defining version remains that of Lawrence Olivier, from 1948. The Mel Gibson *Hamlet* of 1990 possessed an incredible degree of vigour, and was a brilliant adaptation by Franco Zeffirelli.

Verdict: Hamlet is the quintessential Shakespearean play and displays the skills of a writer at the peak of his powers. It is, quite simply, a work of genius. 5/5

The Merry Wives Of Windsor (1600)

> O, what a world of vile ill-favour'd faults looks handsome in
> three hundred pounds a year!

> (Act iii. Sc. 4.)

Story: The story revolves around the attempts of Abraham Slender, cousin of Justice Shallow, and John Falstaff to gain the inheritances of the women of Windsor. Slender wants to marry Anne Page, daughter of Mistress Page, while Falstaff pursues both Mistresses Page and Ford. Mistress Quickly, servant to Doctor Caius, helps both Slender and Fenton, another gentleman, in their pursuit of Anne. Caius, too, wants Anne.

Falstaff sends letters to Ford and Page but they compare them and find they're the same. They plot revenge. Their husbands have also discovered Falstaff's plans and pretend friendship to Falstaff to discover whether he is successful or not. With the help of Quickly, the wives trick Falstaff into false liaisons from which he must escape ignominiously, being dunked and beaten on the way. The wives mend fences with their husbands by showing them the letters and they all conspire one final scheme.

They lure Falstaff to a haunted oak in the forest at midnight and scare the wits out of him. But Fenton has become aware of their plans and makes his own. He spirits Anne away and marries her that night, beating both Slender and Caius. Page, husband and wife, give in to the inevitable and accept the marriage.

Discussion: Falstaff is a great comic creation, ever defeated, ever hopeful and always capable of a brave boast at the end. The play is pure joy and pure farce, on the slimmest of pretexts. It exists only to give these wonderful characters a chance to perform their tricks and traps and, at the end, there is nothing but good feeling. Despite its boisterous comedy, the play is gentle and somewhat wise. It demonstrates how men should trust their wives to be faithful no matter what rumours they hear and how women will always trick and triumph over men.

The dialogue is marvellously balanced and allusive. It is bawdy but never crude, the product of a playwright who is utterly at ease with this comic form. It is, ultimately, a romantic comedy but the romance between Fenton and Anne is a minor part of it. Even though it is the Wives who win, it is the glorious figure of Falstaff who dominates.

Background: The play was probably drawn from some Italian sources but it is difficult to tell because of the amount of invention in it which is wholly attributable to Shakespeare. It is mostly just Shakespeare having fun with one of his favourite characters.

Films: The BBC 1982 version is faithful to the text and tries hard to give full weight to the sheer merriment of the play.

Verdict: Boisterous, joyous and polished, it is the product of a writer at ease and enjoying himself. 5/5

Twelfth Night (1601)

If this were played upon a stage now,
I could condemn it as an improbable fiction.

(Act iii. Sc. 4.)

Story: Viola and Sebastian, lookalike brother and sister, are ship-wrecked and land separately in Illyria. Viola dresses as a man and goes to Duke Orsino's palace, where she finds employment as Orsino's emissary to Olivia, to whom the duke is paying court. Olivia falls in love with the disguised Viola and Viola with Orsino. Malvolio, Olivia's steward, has upset her uncle, Sir Toby Belch, and is tricked by him and her maid, Maria, into believing that Olivia loves him. But when he pays court to her, Olivia has him gaoled as a madman.

Belch also tricks Sir Andrew Aguecheek, another suitor, into a duel with Viola, but this is interrupted by Antonio, who has arrived with his friend Sebastian. Mistaken identities, pursuits and fights follow, and somehow Olivia and Sebastian fall in love then marry immediately.

All the parties meet up at Orsino's palace where, eventually, the mistaken identities are revealed and Orsino declares his love for Viola. Antonio is released, as is Malvolio, and all ends happily.

Discussion: As lightweight as sea foam, it is a splendid comedy of mistaken identity, trickery and knavery. The comic characters are bumptious and full of scope for foolery, and even the fool, for a change, is funny. Sir Toby Belch, in particular, is a wonderful creation, full of plots and plans, and Aguecheek is marvellous as his foil. Malvolio is a wonderfully interesting character, with his self-love and sometimes Puritanism and quite possibly the most complex character in the play.

The inconstancy of love emerges, as Orsino changes his love from Olivia to Viola, and Olivia from Viola to Sebastian. Sebastian, too, seems able to fall in love very quickly, but none of this matters. The play exists to amuse, rather than to investigate the human condition in any sort of depth, and it does this most excellently.

Background: There is an element of Commedia in this play, with Belch and Aguecheek, and some resemblance to an Italian play called *Inganni*. Most of it is the pure invention of Shakespeare, though, and it embodies all the comic tropes which Elizabethan audiences held dear

Films: Trevor Nunn's 1996 adaptation of the play is reasonably faithful, and very well done.

Verdict: A superb comedy. 4/5

Troilus And Cressida (1602)

The common curse of mankind,
—folly and ignorance.

(Act ii. Sc. 3.)

Story: The scene is the siege of Troy, where Troilus is in love with Cressida. She isn't particularly interested in him, despite the efforts of her uncle, Pandarus. Hector, brother of Troilus and the Trojan champion, sends a challenge to Achilles of the Greeks to defend the honour of his mistress but the Greeks arrange that Ajax, another champion, will fight in his stead.

To end the war, Hector urges his father, King Priam, to send Helen, back to the Greeks. Helen, wife of the Greek king Menelaus, was kidnapped by Hector's brother, Paris, thus causing the war. Troilus disagrees, wanting the fight to continue. Pandarus arranges a meeting between Troilus and Cressida, where she admits that she loves him, and Pandarus marries them immediately. However, Calchas, Cressida's father, has arranged to exchange her for a captured Trojan general. Despite protests, the exchange takes place, but Cressida arranges with Troilus to visit her secretly every night in the Greek camp.

The fight between Hector and Ajax takes place but is quickly abandoned, because they discover they are related and do not want to fight to the finish. Hector and Achilles anger each other and arrange to meet on the battlefield the next day. Troilus has fallen in with Ulysses, the wiliest Greek general, who shows him Cressida's infidelity with Diomedes, another general, who Troilus vows to slay.

Battle is joined the next day but Troilus cannot catch Diomedes. Hector kills Patroclus, Achilles' friend, and Achilles, in his turn, kills Hector while he is disarmed. Both parties call a halt to bury their dead and the play ends.

Discussion: Despite the sombre ending, this is a genuine satire. The entire siege of Troy, with its overblown passions and overblown honour, is sent up mercilessly. The great heroes of the Trojan war are shown as human beings rather than the icons they became. Achilles is sulky, Ajax is thick, Ulysses is sly, Hector is overbearingly honourable, Troilus is idiotically romantic and Cressida is a tart. The two great comic creations, who constantly comment on the action, are Pandarus for the Trojans and Thersites for the Greeks. Their acerbic, venal comments bring this epic back to the same ground as Shakespeare's other great comedies; humans and their foibles. This is the forebear of *Up Pompeii* and *Carry On Cleo*.

The theme of the great love between Paris and Helen is mirrored by the love between Troilus and Cressida; passionate, but ephemeral. Despite her protestations of eternal love for Troilus, Cressida doesn't last a full day before she has found another lover.

Background: The story goes back to the *Aenead*, and to Chaucer's version of the same affair.

Films: The BBC produced the play in 1981, and it is their usual faithful rendition.

Verdict: Great comedy, but too drawn out. 4/5

All's Well That Ends Well (1603)

The web of our life is of a mingled yarn,
good and ill together.

(Act iv. Sc. 3.)

Story: The recently widowed French Countess of Rousilon sends her
son, Bertram, to join the king, accompanied by his follower, Parolles.
She later sends her ward, Helena, who is in love with Bertram. Helena,
the daughter of a famous physician, cures the sick king and asks to be
married to Bertram. The king directs this, over Bertram's protests that
Helena is a commoner, but Bertram leaves immediately after the marriage, without consummating it. He goes to the wars in Tuscany and
sends Helena off to his mother. Helena secretly follows him, in disguise, and finds that he is paying court to Diana, who rejects him. Helena proposes an identity swap to consummate her marriage. The ruse is
successful and Bertram heads back to France after receiving a letter
informing him that Helena is dead.

Bertram apologises to the king and attempts to marry the daughter of
Lord Lafeu. Diana arrives and claims that he should marry her because
he slept with her—the treacherous Parolles supports her. Helena arrives
and explains what has happened. Bertram is finally in love with Helena
and the king offers to pay Diana's dowry to any man in the kingdom, so
all are satisfied.

Discussion: For a comedy, this is not a particularly funny play. It has
tragedy and redemption, but the central characters, apart from the
Countess and the king, are hardly admirable. Bertram is a weak, lying
scoundrel who leaves us wondering whether Helena has got a good bargain. Parolles is a braggart in the style of Falstaff, but with none of that
character's humanity or good humour. The scene where Parolles is
brought to book has none of the fun of the similar scene with Falstaff in
Henry IV, Part One but is rather vicious.

The substitution of one woman for another is used in other comedies
but this time it somehow isn't amusing, possibly because we know what

sort of a man Bertram is, and that he doesn't deserve Helena's devotion. The plotting is tight and there's never a dull moment, but the constant build-up of tension is not really relieved by the ending in the king's palace because it doesn't really resolve the conflicts. In the final analysis, we simply find it difficult to believe that Bertram and Helena are going to have a happy marriage.

Background: The story can be found in Boccaccio. As usual, Shakespeare twists it and adds characters like Parolles.

Films: The 1981 BBC Complete works version is a very good one, with Celia Johnson and Ian Charleson in the lead roles.

Verdict: A challenging play, far too serious for a comedy, and far too comic for a drama. Even without classification, difficult to play and difficult to enjoy. 2/5

Othello (1604)

Reputation, reputation, reputation!
Oh, I have lost my reputation!
I have lost the immortal part of myself,
and what remains is bestial.

(Act ii. Sc. 3.)

Story: Othello is a Moorish general in Venice who has made an enemy of Iago, one of his officers. He has also secretly married Desdemona, daughter of Brabantio. Iago informs Brabantio of this, and Othello is brought before the Duke of Venice, but he and Desdemona convince the duke and Brabantio that their love is genuine and receive the duke's blessing.

Othello is sent to Cyprus to fight off a Turkish invasion but by the time he arrives a storm has wiped out their fleet. However, Iago has laid plots to convince Othello that Desdemona, who has accompanied him to Cyprus, is unfaithful. He involves Roderigo, who loves Desdemona, in this and uses him as a cat's-paw in his plans for revenge. He implicates Cassio, Othello's lieutenant, in a brawl and has him stripped of his rank. He then cozens Cassio in the same way he cozened Roderigo.

After planting false evidence, Iago tricks Othello into the belief that Desdemona is having an affair with Cassio. He then tricks Cassio and Roderigo into fighting each other, then wounds Cassio and kills Roderigo in the darkness of the night. Othello believes Cassio dead and confronts Desdemona over her assumed affair, then kills her. Othello is discovered with her body but the plot is revealed, as is Desdemona's innocence. In remorse, Othello kills himself, and then Iago is led away to punishment.

Discussion: Iago is perhaps the most purely villainous of all Shakespeare's villains. At the same time, he is one of the most skilful and cunning, and much of the fascination of the play lies in the way he manipulates those around him. It seems strange that he allows Emilia the power to betray all his hard work.

Like *The Merchant Of Venice*, the final act is almost cursory, having only two scenes, but unlike that play, there is much action in these final scenes. Indeed, the whole play moves quickly, with the focus remaining constantly upon the three main characters; Othello, Desdemona and Iago.

The dialogue is a mixture of blank verse, mostly for Othello and Desdemona, and prose, particularly for Iago. Iago, indeed, spends a great deal of his time explaining his thoughts to the audience in asides, a return to a much older tradition of the theatrical villain.

Background: Most likely drawn from a story of Cinthio, a real Moor in the service of Venice, the play takes a very mundane story and makes it into a genuine and compelling tragedy.

Films: The 1995 film with Kenneth Branagh and Laurence Fishburne is a spectacular adaptation, but the best performance is the 1965 film, with a superb cast, including Laurence Olivier as the Moor.

Verdict: Despite Iago, there are too many characters who act foolishly and give the play something of a contrived air. Iago is certainly a master puppeteer but the strings linking him to his puppets are strained. 3/5

Measure For Measure (1604)

Some rise by sin, and some by virtue fall.

(Act ii. Sc. 1.)

Story: Duke Vincenzio of Vienna leaves the city for a while, handing over government to Angelo, his deputy. Angelo imposes a strict rule of law in Vincenzio's absence. He arrests Claudio, a gentleman, for making Juliet pregnant and closes the brothels, depriving Mistress Overdone of clientele.

Claudio had intended to marry Juliet and he asks his friend Lucio to try to have his death sentence repealed. Lucio, in turn, seeks aid from Claudio's sister, Isabella. When Isabella pleads with Angelo, he lusts after her and asks her to sleep with him to save her brother. She refuses and he threatens to torture Claudio unless she accedes.

The duke returns, disguised as a friar and sees Juliet led away to prison. He discovers her offence and that of Claudio, and acts as adviser to Claudio. When he discovers Angelo's threat, he advises Isabella to give in then swap identities with another woman, one who Angelo once refused to marry, despite being betrothed.

Vincenzio returns without disguise and hears petitioners. He hears Isabella and then Mariana, the woman with whom she swapped identities. After more deception, in which Lucio unwittingly reveals the duke as the friar, Vincenzio marries Angelo to Mariana, Claudio to Juliet, Lucio to Overdone (for having made her pregnant many years ago) and then he marries Isabella. The play ends in a sea of matrimony.

Discussion: Many plots and disguises, somewhat dark, but none of the characters really attract our sympathy. Too many of them are sophisticates and the love affair between Claudio and Juliet is so sketchily described that it almost passes us by. Mistress Overdone is the closest thing to a sympathetic character but she appears too briefly. While the other characters are, at times, amusing, there is little of the warmth that characterises the best of Shakespeare's comedies.

The theme that those who wish to impose virtue must be virtuous in themselves does not really seem to work. Angelo was tempted by Isabella, where he had previously been upright, although a prig. His rejection of Mariana was legal, after all, and moral, if somewhat less than sensitive. The duke makes no pretence at Angelo's objectivity, even though he describes himself as virtuous to Lucio when in disguise. The corruption in Vienna was, he admits, worse before he left. Perhaps the final message of the play is that it is better to be governed by people, with all their failings, rather than by the cold majesty of the law.

Background: Almost certainly, the play was drawn from George Whetstone's play *Promos And Cassandra*, which was drawn from Giraldi Cinthio's *Hecatomitthi*.

Films: The 1979 BBC production does a surprisingly good job of staging one of Shakespeare's more difficult plays.

Verdict: Not the best of comedies. Some of the scenes drag on for far too long, and the revelations in the fifth act seem to take forever, only to close too rapidly with all the issues resolved within some fifty lines. 3/5

King Lear (1605)

The worst is not so long as we can say, "This is the worst."

(Act iv. Sc. 1.)

Story: King Lear intends to retire and divide his kingdom between his three daughters, Goneril, Regan and Cordelia. When he thinks Cordelia does not show him sufficient respect, he deprives her of her third and splits it between the other two. Lear's closest adviser, Kent, warns him against this and is banished. Cordelia leaves with a suitor, the King of France, who still loves her even though she is landless. In the meantime Edmund, the Duke of Gloucester's bastard son, is plotting to displace Edgar, the legitimate son. He is successful in convincing Gloucester that Edgar means to kill him, and Edgar runs off.

Even though Kent has disguised himself and joined Lear to protect him, the situation rapidly worsens. Lear is quickly deprived of all men, honours and respect he feels he is due and goes mad. He runs out into a storm, accompanied only by his Fool. Kent chases after and catches them but cannot convince Lear to return. Gloucester attempts to intercede with Cornwall, Regan's husband, but is warned not to speak of the matter. When Gloucester receives a letter from the King of France asking assistance, Edmund betrays him to Cornwall, who puts out Gloucester's eyes but is killed by a servant when he does.

Lear has been joined by Edgar, disguised as a madman, while Gloucester wanders the countryside. Edmund makes love to both sisters and France invades. Eventually, battle is joined between England and France, and England is victorious, capturing Lear and Cordelia who are with the French. Albany, Goneril's husband, allows a single combat between Edmund and Edgar because he has discovered Edmund's affairs. Goneril and Regan kill each other and Gloucester dies off stage. Edgar kills Edmund, who warns them that an assassin has been sent after Lear and Cordelia. The warning is too late because Cordelia is dead. Lear dies soon after.

Discussion: The mistake was Lear's, to upset the apple cart by giving up the burden of kingship before death. This he compounded by trusting flatterers, rather than his plain-speaking daughter Cordelia. This disturbance to the natural order of things must be redressed but it gets worse before it gets better, with Goneril and Regan acting against nature as well. The storm in act III mirrors the way that nature is turned upside down, and it is only when the natural order begins to be restored that the storm, both natural and political, begins to abate.

Edmund is one of Shakespeare's finest villains. He is utterly unscrupulous, yet courageous and, in many ways, charming. His speech about his bastardry is one of the finest in all of the canon and expresses his vigour both of thought and action. At the end, he acts nobly, since he does not have to fight Edgar, nor does he have to reveal the threat to Lear and Cordelia. A most sympathetic villain.

Background: The source for *King Lear* is Holinshed's *Chronicles*, although the end differs. In Holinshed, Lear goes to France, both dukes are killed in battle, then Lear is restored to the throne and reigns for two years. Cordelia also becomes queen and reigns for five years, before being imprisoned by her nephews and committing suicide.

Films: There have been many attempts to translate *King Lear* onto both large and small screens, with varying degrees of success. The best versions are probably the 1971 film, directed by Peter Brook and starring Paul Scofield, and the 1984 television production, directed by Michael Elliot and starring Laurence Olivier. Akira Kurosawa based *Ran* on the play, and this version, while it changes some elements significantly, is superb.

Verdict: Often considered to be Shakespeare's other greatest tragedy, *King Lear* is almost operatic in nature. Everything is on a very grand scale. However, Edgar and Cordelia are almost too good, upright and honest to ring true. The villains seem somehow far more easily understood. 5/5

Macbeth (1606)

But screw your courage to the sticking-place,
and we'll not fail.

(Act i. Sc. 7.)

Story: Macbeth and Banquo, lords of Scotland on their way home
from battle, meet three witches who prophesy that Macbeth will be
king, and Banquo begetter of kings, although not king himself. This
prophecy begins to come true almost immediately, when Duncan, the
King of Scotland, makes Macbeth the Thane of Cawdor. Lady Macbeth
receives a letter informing her of the prophecy, and immediately plans
to make it come true, by murdering Duncan, who is intending to stay at
their castle. She convinces Macbeth to do this and they try to pin the
murder on Malcolm, Duncan's son and heir. He runs away to England
so Macbeth becomes king.

To ensure his safety, Macbeth has Banquo murdered, but his ghost
returns to a banquet, unsettling Macbeth, who is the only one to see
him. Macbeth seeks reassurance from the witches and they tell him no
man born of woman can harm him and that he is safe until Birnam
Wood comes to Dunsinane, his castle.

Malcolm raises an army in England, aided by Macduff, another lord.
Macbeth murders Macduff's family, and Macduff swears revenge.
Macbeth's excesses have begun to lose him followers, whilst Lady
Macbeth is driven mad by guilt and dies of it. Malcolm attacks, cutting
the trees of Birnam Wood to disguise his army, thus fulfilling one of the
witches' prophecies. Macbeth seems untouchable until confronted by
Macduff, who reveals that he was "ripped untimely from his mother's
womb." They fight. Macduff kills Macbeth, then throws his head at the
feet of Malcolm, confirming him as unchallenged King of Scotland.

Discussion: Full of the supernatural, treachery, murder and battle,
Macbeth is engrossing drama. The tragedy of Macbeth, who begins as a
faithful servant of his king but who is seduced by his own ambitions, is
a compelling one. Even though he descends to murder and tyranny,

there is still some relic of nobility about him when he warns off Macduff and when he accepts Macduff's challenge, as if he has not quite allowed evil to totally destroy the man he once was.

It sometimes seems that Shakespeare could not avoid putting fine words in the mouths of villains and he does so with Macbeth. His bitter reflections on life and what it has led him to, reveal the humanity beneath the monster, eloquently expressing his hopelessness. Neither Malcolm nor Macduff have speeches as fine, and Malcolm, in truth, is a somewhat anaemic character when compared with Macbeth.

Background: Macbeth was a historic figure, although he reigned in Scotland for seventeen years, not for the few weeks which Shakespeare allows him. The story can be found, once more, in Holinshed's *Chronicles,* although his Macbeth is less evil than in the play, and his Duncan somewhat less innocent.

Films: Polanski's 1971 *Macbeth,* with a dynamic performance from Jon Finch, is by far the best rendition of the play on film, although Orson Welles' 1948 black and white version comes close.

Verdict: It is one of Shakespeare's finest tragedies. 5/5

Antony And Cleopatra (1607)

Age cannot wither her,
nor custom stale her infinite variety.

(Act ii. Sc. 2.)

Story: Antony is in Alexandria, besotted with Cleopatra, when he receives news that his wife, Fulvia, has died after rebelling against Octavius, another member of the ruling triumvirate of Rome. He returns to Rome, where Octavius and Lepidus, the third member of the triumvirate, berate him for his indulgence in Egypt, but the three are reconciled to fight Pompey, a rebellious general. Antony accepts Octavia, Octavius' sister, in marriage, and they leave to combat Pompey.

A diplomatic solution is achieved with Pompey and the revolt in the East is settled. Antony goes to live with Octavia in Athens, but cannot stay there. He declares war on Octavius, raises a fleet and an army, and returns to Cleopatra. Octavius forces Antony into a sea battle, which is lost because Cleopatra runs away and takes the Egyptian fleet with her. Despite this betrayal, Antony cannot part from her.

Antony defeats Octavius on land but loses another seas battle, under the same circumstances as the first, and all is lost. Cleopatra runs from his wrath and hides in her burial monument, sending back word that she's dead. When he hears this, Antony kills himself, asking to be laid next to her and dies in her arms. Cleopatra cannot bear to be a prisoner and kills herself by clasping a snake to her bosom.

Discussion: A tangled story of statecraft and passion. We are confronted by a man very much of the world, who has demonstrated his martial and political abilities following the death of Julius Caesar, twisted around the finger of a rather manipulative woman. For love, he gives up everything, forgives every crime and, finally, kills himself. It is a classical tragedy, in that the fall of a great man is brought about by his own weakness, one to which he is largely blind. Even Octavius regrets the necessity for Antony's death. Octavius is a noble character, one in full control of himself, just and merciful, but willing to sacrifice even those he admires for the good of Rome.

Cleopatra is passion embodied, which may be why Antony finds her so attractive. But she also is a victim of her passion and cannot carry through her plans to support Antony. She seems weak and is only barely redeemed by the nobility of her death. Overwhelmingly, though, she gives the impression of frivolity and instability, which are not good qualities in anyone who would war with Rome.

Background: The story comes from Plutarch, but Shakespeare has largely ignored the Cleopatra presented there to create his own. More passionate and less politically acute; sexier, but less clever. It follows on from *Julius Caesar* and there are several references to that play.

Films: One of the more popular plays for filming, the Taylor/Burton version was glorious and grand, but not particularly faithful to the play. The 1981 BBC version is quite faithful to the play, but less gorgeous.

Verdict: Too long, too scattered, the play gives the impression of being a patchwork. There is far too much jumping around from scene to scene, and there are odds and ends left unresolved. The major characters of Antony and Cleopatra never seem to really gel. 3/5

Coriolanus (1608)

Nature teaches beasts to know their friends.

(Act ii. Sc. 1.)

Story: Coriolanus is a Roman senator who has lost the approval of the people by his high-handed attitude towards them. They believe that he is keeping food from them in a time of famine. He leaves these things behind and goes away to fight the Volscians, which he does with great personal courage, only just failing to kill their leader, Aufidius. Because of his courage and generalship, he is proposed as Consul. Despite his triumph over the Volscians, the people refuse to confirm him as Consul, partly because a tribune, Junius Brutus, has reminded them of his disdain.

Coriolanus hears this news and curses the people and the Roman political system. He is accused of treason as a result. When the tribunes attempt to arrest him, he draws his sword and occasions a riot, during which he escapes. Menenius, his friend, and Volumnia, his mother, plead with him to face the people and retract his statements. He does, but loses his temper when accused of treason and is banished.

He joins with Aufidius, the Volscian general he had previously defeated, and they raise an army to conquer Rome. When the citizens of Rome hear this, they regret their previous decision and attempt to make amends. Coriolanus, though, is refusing all messengers, and does not hear their pleas until Volumnia and Virgilia, his wife, plead with him. He marches the army away to Antium, where Aufidius kills him for not carrying out their plan to sack Rome, finally avenging his many defeats at Coriolanus' hands.

Discussion: Coriolanus is probably the most unsympathetic of Shakespeare's heroes. He is proud, disdainful and hates the common person with a passion. Yet it is undeniable that he has served Rome well, saved her from defeat and put his own body between her and her enemies. What part of the man should we then value most? This is the question the play asks. For his accomplishments, Coriolanus was undoubtedly worthy of a consulship, but he was not popular. His unpopularity was at least partly fomented by the tribunes. What is the opinion of the people worth? They are shown to be fickle, forgetful and faithless, bowing to the last person to talk to them, as long as that person tells them what they want to hear. They are shown to have no appreciation of honesty and less gratitude. While Coriolanus may be disdainful, he comes off in a better light than the people who dragged him down.

This is a tragedy in the sense that a great man's fault destroyed him but, unlike most of the tragedies, Coriolanus was well aware of his fault and saw it as a central part of his character. It is, perhaps, in our egalitarian world, difficult to feel sympathy for him, but it is also a reflection on the way the crowd in Shakespeare's time, and today, can make or break a man of worth who does not sing them the right song. As we do today, the Romans wound up with the government they deserved.

Background: The story is drawn from Plutarch with some contemporary references.

Films: The 1984 BBC version is quite good, with Alan Howard as Coriolanus, as is the 1979 US version with Morgan Freeman in the title role.

Verdict: The play has a certain power, but Coriolanus is too distant a character. Since he dominates the play, the play itself becomes distant, despite its intelligence. 3/5

Timon Of Athens (1608)

Nothing emboldens sin so much as mercy.

(Act iii. Sc. 5.)

Story: Timon seems filthy rich, surrounded by false friends and flatterers. The truth is that he is just about bankrupt, but refuses to admit it. When his creditors call in their debts, his erstwhile friends refuse to help him. He holds one last ironic banquet for them, where he feasts them on lukewarm water, and discovers that perhaps his only true friend, the warrior Alcibiades, has been banished for manslaughter. He drives out his false friends and leaves Athens to live as a hermit.

Timon shelters in a cave and, while digging for roots, stumbles across a vast treasure. He offers money to Alcibiades, to aid him in conquering Athens, which Alcibiades accepts and leaves to raise an army. When two thieves come by, Timon gives them gold, and encourages them to steal. When word of Timon's new-found wealth reaches Athens, they offer him the leadership of the city, but he rejects their offer. Alcibiades conquers Athens and sends for Timon, but he is dead and a soldier brings the epitaph he wrote back to Athens.

Discussion: It's hard to find redeeming features in this play. Timon is the core of it, and a nastier, more unattractive character would be hard to find in all of Shakespeare, and he's not even a villain. The themes are obvious—the fruits of ingratitude and how silly it is to trust bought friends—but the plot is ludicrous. The accidental discovery of gold outside Timon's cave is not explained in any way. It's just there. His death is unexplained. He just dies, possibly of choler. There are really no other characters who get much of a look-in and most of Timon's later speeches are simply ranting.

Background: The story is drawn from Plutarch with some contribution from Lucian. The text of the play is not good and seems to be notes rather than finished text. It was in the first folio but put in the space for *Troilus And Cressida*. Something of a dog's breakfast.

Films: Jonathan Price is a brilliant Timon in this 1981 BBC production, and the entire cast work hard to make something of a terrible script.

Verdict: Terrible. Unfinished and almost unplayable. 1/5

Pericles (1608)

Truth can never be confirmed enough,
though doubts did ever sleep.

(Act v, sc. 1.)

Story: Pericles has guessed a riddle and earned the King of Antioch's daughter, but the king plans to kill Pericles first. Pericles flees back to Tyre, but a hired killer, Thaliard, follows him. Helicanus, a trusted lord, urges him to flee again and he runs to Tarsus.

Despite earning the gratitude of the Cleon, the Governor of Tarsus, by alleviating a famine, Pericles must flee again because Thaliard is following him. Pericles is shipwrecked off Pentapolis, survives and wins the hand of the King Simonides' daughter, Thaisa. He receives a message that the King of Antioch and his daughter are dead, and heads back to Tyre. On the way, a storm apparently kills Thaisa in childbirth and she's buried at sea. However, she was merely in a trance and is washed up on the shore of Ephesus and revived by Lord Cerimon. Pericles leaves their daughter, Marina, to be raised by Cleon, in Tarsus.

When Marina has reached adulthood, Cleon's wife, Dionyza, becomes jealous of her and plans to have her killed but Marina falls into the hands of pirates, who sell her to a brothel keeper in Mytilene. When Pericles arrives in Tarsus, they tell him Marina is dead and he falls into grief. In Mytilene, Marina proves too virtuous for the brothel and escapes it by opening a school.

Pericles visits Mytilene, and Lysimachus, the Governor, sends Marina to cure him of his melancholy. He recognises her and then the goddess Diana reveals that Thaisa is a votress in a temple nearby. Pericles hurries there, regains Thaisa and betroths Marina to Lysimachus. Diomedes has died and Pericles leaves to take the throne, leaving Lysimachus and Marina the rule of Tyre.

Discussion: Part of the problem with this play is that the text is a poor one. It wasn't included in the first Folio of 1623 for lack of a decent script. Even with a good text, though, it is difficult to see how this vast chain of coincidence and mischance could be knitted together. Quite simply, too much happens in too short a space of time, which makes the play episodic, and somewhat incoherent. With all the uncertainty of the text, what we have now is a sketch of a play, which does little justice to the story.

The characters are effortlessly eloquent. There is, however, no let up from their eloquence; even the brothel keepers are serious and intent. Perhaps, in the end, it is that there is no relief from this intensity which makes the play so difficult to enjoy. If ever a play cried out for a modern rewrite to film, this one does. The adventure story is epic in scale and would be grand on the big screen.

Background: Like Odysseus, the Pericles of legend went through many adventures and the story itself goes back to Apollonius of Tyre.

Films: The BBC production of 1984 tries hard to make this work on the small screen.

Verdict: Not the bard's finest work, too episodic and disjointed. 2/5

Cymbeline (1609)

Some griefs are medicinable.

(Act iii. Sc. 2)

Story: Imogen has married Posthumus, against the wishes of her
father, Cymbeline, King of Britain. Posthumus has been banished and
winds up in Rome, where he bets Iachomo, an Italian friend, that Imogen will remain virtuous while he's away. Iachomo goes to England and
tries to seduce Imogen but fails. He does, however, manage to hide in a
trunk she agrees to store in her bedroom for him. He steals a bracelet
from her and this, along with his description of the bedroom, is enough
to win the bet for him when he returns to Rome.

Cloten, the stepson of Cymbeline, pays court to Imogen, but she also
rejects him. Posthumus, meanwhile, has seen the evidence from
Iachomo and wants revenge on Imogen. He sends her a letter via
Pisanio, a faithful retainer, to meet him at Milford Haven but he has
instructed Pisanio to kill her when she gets there.

An ambassador from Rome, Lucien, has arrived in England to
demand tribute, but Cymbeline has refused and war is imminent. When
Pisanio finds he can't kill Imogen, he suggests she disguise herself as a
man and join Lucien's entourage. Cloten discovers Imogen's where-
abouts and goes after her but Imogen has fallen in with three outlaws,
Belarius, Guiderius and Aviragus; the latter two are unknown sons of
Cymbeline and the first is a wrongfully banished lord who has raised
them as his own. Imogen is sick from a poison and seems to die. The
boys find Cloten and kill him.

Cymbeline goes to battle against the Romans, joined by Beliarus and
the boys. Posthumus is with the Romans, seeking death now that he has
received a letter from Pisanio that explains the truth. In the battle, Cymbeline is eventually triumphant, but the Queen has died, confessing that
she attempted to poison Imogen. At the end, Belarius comes out of disguise and reveals the two boys as Cymbeline's sons, and Posthumus

and Imogen are reunited. To avoid further pointless conflict, Cymbeline decides to pay the tribute to Rome.

Discussion: This is a long play and one which seems to have no turning. There are scene changes for no apparent purpose but to give a character a long speech, and the last scene is unconscionably long, seemingly in order to resolve everything.

The theme of mistaken revenge on a supposedly errant wife is one familiar from *Othello*, and that of the good lord exiled by an ill-advised monarch is similar to *King Lear*. The woman disguised as a man is from any number of plays, and the bet about a wife's chastity is straight out of his poem *The Rape Of Lucrece*. The whole play gives the impression of being cobbled together out of spare parts.

There is still wonderful language in this play. The funeral oration over the supposedly dead Imogen is some of Shakespeare's finest dramatic poetry. The vicious asides of the lords who accompany Cloten are some of Shakespeare's wittiest. The dialogue really has no faults but it seems a pity it was wasted on such a play as this.

Background: Holinshed, again, with influence from sources such as Spenser's *The Faerie Queene*, but with many references to Shakespeare's other plays. Cymbeline actually was a king, but his real name was Cunobelinus.

Films: The 1983 BBC production, with a stellar cast including Helen Mirren and Claire Bloom, does great service to a very average play.

Verdict: Far too long, and in need of a good editor. It is a failed experiment, but a worthy one. 2/5

The Winter's Tale (1610)

To unpathed waters, undreamed shores.

(Act iv. Sc. 4.)

Story: Leontes, the King of Sicily, becomes convinced his wife, Hermione, is having an affair with his old friend Polyxenes, of Bohemia. He assigns a lord, Camillo, to murder him but Camillo can't do it, smuggles Polyxenes out of the city and goes to Bohemia with him. Leontes, hearing this, descends further into madness and imprisons Hermione.

Hermione has a girl baby in prison but Leontes directs another lord, Antigonus, to leave it in the desert to die. He tries Hermione for treason and condemns her to death. He defies Apollo to do this and his son, Mamillus, dies. Hermione faints and dies. Antigonus leaves the child Perdita in the desert and is killed by a bear. Perdita is found by a shepherd and raised as his daughter.

After Hermione's death, Leontes recovers from his madness and sixteen years pass. Polixenes' son, Florizel, is paying court to Perdita and Camillo wants to return home to die. Polyxenes warns Florizel off but, with the help and advice of Camillo, he and Perdita go to Sicily. At the court of Leontes, Perdita is recognised as his daughter and the wedding between Florizel and Perdita is sanctioned by Polyxenes. Leontes is reunited with Hermione, who has been under a magical spell as a statue for the last sixteen years, until her daughter returned to her.

Discussion: Straightforward and charming, the play doesn't waste time getting through the story. The characters are much more successful than its immediate predecessor, *Cymbeline*, and Perdita, in particular, is a wonderful creation. Leontes' madness leaves as quickly as it arrived, but this remains, somehow, believable. In the later acts, his remorse is quite authentic, as is his joy at the resurrected Hermione.

There is much good poetry in the play, particularly that of Autolycus, a friend of Florizel's. He is also a great comic creation, much in the tradition of Falstaff. The theme of jealousy and its effects has appeared in

Othello and other plays, but it is treated more gently here. The old theme of class difference also arises but the dilemma it causes is solved rapidly.

Background: The play is mostly drawn from Robert Greene's novel, *Pandosto*, but there are, as always, the inventions of Shakespeare's fruitful mind. Autolycus is the most successful of these and contributes much to the charm of the play.

Films: The 1981 BBC version is just about the only one available, although there was a better production in 1961 with Robert Shaw.

Verdict: All charm, eminently playable and eminently watchable, it's a pity it is not produced more often. 4/5

The Tempest (1611)

Oh brave new world, that has such creatures in it.

(Act v, Sc. 1)

Story: Prospero, the rightful Duke of Milan, has been washed up on a small island with his daughter Miranda after his brother Antonio usurped his rule. After many years have passed, Prospero, through his magic, brings to the island a ship with Antonio, Alonso (the King of Milan), Ferdinand (his son), Sebastian (Alonso's brother) and Gonzalo (the aged advisor who saved Prospero and Miranda when they were set adrift in a small boat).

Prospero, through his captive spirit, Ariel, manipulates events so that Ferdinand meets and falls in love with Miranda. He then forces him to prove his worth by doing menial tasks. The others, again by Ariel's intervention, are led around in circles. In another part of the island, Trinculo and Stephano, two servants, meet up with Caliban, son of the witch Sycorax and the original inhabitant of the island, and plot with him to kill Prospero and take control. First, Caliban tells them, they must steal Prospero's books.

While Caliban, Trinculo and Stephano get drunk, Alonso and his group are led to Prospero's cell, where he reveals himself to them. He explains how he came to the island but forgives Antonio, requiring only that he be given back his dukedom. The love between Miranda and Ferdinand is sealed and receives Alonso's blessing. After dispensing with Caliban's attack, all situations are resolved. Trinculo and Stephano are forgiven, Ariel is released from bondage and Caliban will be left the island after Prospero leaves.

Prospero gives up his books, his staff and all his powers to return to Milan, "where every third thought shall be my grave." He will return to the world for a short time before leaving it forever.

Discussion: One of the shortest of Shakespeare's plays, *The Tempest* revolves around the central figure of Prospero. This character study of Prospero is fascinating. The man of power who, having achieved his ends, forgives his enemies and gives up his power is a complex character and a continuing intellectual challenge.

As one of the last, if not the very last, of Shakespeare's plays, it has often been seen as his farewell to the theatre. There are certainly parallels in Prospero to the way in which a writer/director controls the stage and creates illusions for the audience. There are also allusions to the stage in some of the speeches and the epilogue begs the audience to release him through their approval of what he has wrought. If it is the last play, then it is a fitting valedictory to the greatest of English dramatists.

Background: The story is drawn from that of *The Venture*, a ship which was wrecked near Bermuda, yet without loss of life. The play is full of allusions to the New World and the discoveries made there, both real and fanciful.

Films: The 1980 BBC production does not use a good cast to advantage, but the lines are relatively clear, and they're all there. Derek Jarman's 1979 production is less faithful but it is utterly gorgeous and evokes the magical spirit of the play.

Verdict: Complex, challenging and difficult to play, perhaps too complex for the stage, as some music is too complex to be played. 4/5

Henry VIII (1613)

`Tis better to be lowly born,
and range with humble livers in content,
than to be perked up in a glistering grief,
and wear a golden sorrow.

(Act ii. Sc. 3.)

Story: Henry is married to Katherine but the marriage isn't happy and there are plots against the throne. Cardinal Wolsey is chief among the plotters, using his office to eliminate rivals for Henry's favours. Henry meets Anne Bullen at a party held by Wolsey and falls in love with her. This causes relations with Katherine to become even worse and Wolsey plays on his conscience to get rid of her, justifying it because she was the wife of Henry's dead brother.

Katherine is outmanoeuvred by Wolsey and exiled from Court. Henry makes Anne the Marchioness of Pembroke in preparation for asking for her hand. He has no male heir, which he blames on Katherine, and suspects that their marriage may be invalid because of her previous marriage to his brother, which could cause problems with the succession. When he puts this question to his councillors at law, they cannot prove his marriage legitimate and he has his marriage to Katherine annulled.

Against the wishes of Wolsey, he marries Anne. He finds that Wolsey, as Chancellor of England, has been fiddling the books to acquire enough money to make himself Pope, so Henry removes him from office. Henry makes the marriage to Anne public, at which Katherine falls ill and dies. Wolsey follows soon after. Anne gives birth to a girl, the future Queen Elizabeth, and the play ends with an oration from Cranmer, the Archbishop of Canterbury, regarding the bright future the child will have.

Discussion: The last of Shakespeare's history plays, and probably his last play, *Henry VIII* is distinct in some ways from those written before. There are no wars, for a start, and the stage directions for this play are more complete than for any other play. It is very much a play of pomp and spectacle, which is one of the reasons for the stage directions. It is also a play of many long speeches; there is little of the patter which is present in most other plays. This gives the play a heavy dignity which at times verges on the ponderous.

Henry is shown in a much more favourable light than history allows him. The play wisely stops with the birth of Elizabeth, shortly after his marriage to Anne, and leaves out his four other wives. Anne, too, is treated very generously. Indeed, there seems to be hardly a villain in the play. Even Wolsey repents after being discovered and confined, and gives up all his possessions to the king.

That is the great fault with the play. It treads far too lightly on the grave of Henry. There is none of the boisterous humour or high emotion which Shakespeare could command so easily. There is nothing in this play which will wring the heart. The dialogue is masterful, as would be expected of someone who is long past petty errors, but empty. Still, there are great pageants, masques and processions, and the splendour of court.

Background: Shakespeare had little need to go to sources other than recent records and the memories of those who had lived through Henry's reign, or their children.

Films: Claire Bloom starred as Katherine in the 1979 BBC production and is excellent in the part, and the rest of the play is a useful interpretation.

Verdict: Skilled and empty, the play is a disappointment, a shy chronicle of a powerful king. 2/5

Poems

Shakespeare wrote four long poems, *A Lover's Complaint, Venus And Adonis, The Phoenix And The Turtle* and *The Rape Of Lucrece* and 154 Sonnets. The Sonnets, along with *Venus And Adonis* and *The Rape Of Lucrece* were written under the patronage of Henry Wriothesly, the Earl of Southampton. Many of the Sonnets directly concerned Wriothesly and his tangled affairs. Many related directly to Shakespeare's own love life. While there is equal poetry in the plays, the Sonnets do more to reveal Shakespeare, the man, to us than any other text.

A Lover's Complaint (1591)

This is the witty account of a young maid who has been seduced and abandoned, as she tells the episode to a priest who has discovered her ridding herself of the remnants of the affair in a river. She tells of how she protested her innocence to the seducer but eventually succumbed to his honeyed tongue and his protestation of love for her. As she tells the priest, she knew of the man's reputation but believed his lies when he told her that she was different, that she was more beautiful than jewels and when he wept for love of her. The maid regrets that she "fell" but archly admits to the priest that she'd probably do it again for such a lover. Light-hearted and lightweight, the poem is simply a five-finger exercise for a poet trying his wings off stage, and a very successful one.

Verdict: 3/5

Venus And Adonis (1593)

This is also light in weight but was written for a different purpose. It tells the classic story of the beautiful Adonis, who is indifferent to women, even to the charm of Venus, the Goddess of Love, herself. Adonis is out hunting one day and Venus attempts to seduce him, offering him Olympian delights if he'll dally with her. She is so taken with the lad that she drags him from his horse and pushes him to the ground, fawns upon him and caresses him, but the boy isn't having any. When she begs for a kiss, he spurns her again, though she reminds him that even the gods have lusted for her.

Her pleas, her beauty and her offers of immortal delights have no effect on the self-impressed youth. She tells him what a waste it is that he's not using the beautiful body he possesses for the purpose which nature intended it. When a beautiful young mare trots into their glade and his horse breaks its tether and goes after it in lust, she points out that this is how he should be behaving.

Nothing works. All Adonis wants to do is hunt. He's too young for all this, he tells her, even though he's not too young to go hunting boars. Finally, she pretends to faint and he's worried that he has killed her by denying her what she wants. First, he slaps her cheek to bring her around, then kisses her. At that she rises up but he's not prepared to go any farther. One more kiss as a fee for parting and he wants to be off to hunt boar. Venus holds onto him, warns him of the dangers of this occupation and advises him to hunt hares instead. She holds him until night, while he abuses her for not being the right sort of love, then he breaks away and runs off into the darkness.

Venus, in the dawn, hears the hunters out after boar again. She knows that there's going to be trouble and runs after them. She's right, as one might expect of a goddess, and finds the boar, emerging from the brush with a bloody snout. She comes across the torn and mangled body of Adonis. He fought the boar and the boar won. Venus laments his death and prophecies, somewhat churlishly, that love shall, forever after, be full of sorrow. In a final gesture, and one somewhat beloved of Greek Gods, she turns his body into a flower, the purple anemone, which she plucks and tucks between her breasts, just to remind her of the beautiful youth whose innocence she could not conquer.

Wriothesly was somewhat ambivalent in his sexual preferences and Shakespeare was attempting to show him what happened to people who couldn't make up their minds who to love. Eventually, the poem points out, such love is really love of self and produces nothing. The genius of Shakespeare is to do so in such a bawdy, sensual, entertaining fashion. The portrait of Venus as a somewhat dizzy, lovestruck bimbo, very miffed that her charms won't work on Adonis, is masterly. Adonis himself is conceited and something of a prat, being far too upright for his own good. Venus' mourning of his death is just too much, and there are hints that her final determination to cloister herself away from the world may not last. There are many lines in the poem which are, to say the least, suggestive, yet the artfulness of the language is such that they are always amusing, rather than seamy.

Verdict: 4/5

The Rape Of Lucrece (1594)

This is the serious work that Shakespeare promised his patron at the time of *Venus And Adonis*. Nearly twice as long, there is no humour in this poem. Again, the story is a classic one, drawn from Roman history. It is dark and brooding. There are some digressions which appear unnecessary but they do not detract from the intensity of the story. Rather, they add to the tension, by delaying the inevitable.

Collatine's wife, Lucrece, is a model of virtue. Tarquin, a son of the ruling family of Rome, becomes infatuated with Lucrece and slips away to visit her. His intentions are not honourable—they are evil.

Lucrece welcomes him as a Roman matron should, with courtesy and generosity. After dinner, she sees Tarquin to his bed but he can't sleep for his thoughts of her. Tormented by his passion, he waits until all are asleep, then gets up and creeps to Lucrece's chamber. All the way there, he debates with himself the action he is about to take, honour and lust warring within him. Lust wins.

He enters the chamber and sees her asleep, naked, on the bed. All thoughts of honour vanish. He wakes her and, at first, attempts to talk her into surrendering to him. He threatens her and tells her that, if she makes a fuss, he'll rape her anyway, then kill her and one of her servants, telling the world that he discovered the servant in her bed, thereby destroying her honour and that of Collatine, as well as taking her life. She pleads with him, using all the arguments at her command, but to no avail. He gags her with her sheets and rapes her.

Sated, wracked by guilt, Tarquin steals away in the night. His re-awakened conscience tells him the enormity of his deed. Lucrece is distraught, caught between honour and vengeance. She feels guilty and angry and vengeful but worries about the opinion of others, how they might believe she encouraged Tarquin in some way. She curses Tarquin roundly, wishing upon him every disaster she can imagine but can only see one way out of her dilemma.

She sends a messenger for Collatine, who arrives quickly, with other lords in attendance, including Lucrece's father, Lucretius. Lucrece tells them the story of what happened, detailing how her hospitality was betrayed, how she was blackmailed, how she was raped but holds back Tarquin's name until the very last. Despite the protests of her husband, father and the lords that her honour is unstained, that she has no guilt, she tells them that no one will ever use her name as a reason for giving in to another's lusts. With that she reveals Tarquin as the rapist, draws a dagger and stabs herself before anyone can stop her, to prove her story with her life.

The lords are stunned and dismayed by her action. They lament her death but soon embark on her revenge. They bear her bleeding body through Rome, publishing Tarquin's deed and he is banished forever.

Despite its length, *The Rape Of Lucrece* is stunning poetry. The steamy, dark atmosphere of lust, betrayal and death is evoked so that one can almost feel it. The portrayal of Lucrece as she comes to her tortured decision to kill herself, her feelings of guilt and her distractedness are anguishing. While some critics have seen the poem as somewhat overdone, it remains one which has, perhaps, greater appeal to the modern mind than the other long poems.

Verdict: 4/5

The Phoenix And The Turtle (1601)

This is the last of Shakespeare's non-dramatic poems, and by far the shortest, at only 67 lines. It was published in 1601 as a contribution to a book by Robert Chester, *Love's Martyr*. While the book was intended to celebrate a happy marriage, that of Sir John Salisbury and his wife Ursula, the poem looks more at the death of love than its life. The 'turtle' of the title is not the one with the shell, but the turtledove, and the poem tells of how the love between the two birds eventually consumes them both in the flames of the phoenix. There is one passage that indicates that this may also have been aimed at Wriothesly, who was then confined to the Tower of London under sentence of death for the part he played in the Essex Rebellion. It says that the birds left no children, not because of their infirmity, but because of 'married chastity.'

Short, simple and to the point, the poem has a gemlike quality and is far more symbolic and allusive than the other, more narrative poems. However, while it is skilful, it seems to lack the heart of the others.

Verdict: 3/5

The Sonnets

So long as men can breathe or eyes can see
So long lives this, and this gives life to thee.

Sonnet 18

The Sonnets were written in the years 1592 to 1595 and are Shakespeare's greatest poetic achievement. While he did not invent the form, in these poems he made it his own, and the particular rhyme scheme used has become identified with him as the Shakespearean Sonnet. They were largely written during a period when the plague had struck London, in 1592–1593, and the theatres had been closed. Topical references show that Shakespeare continued to write them until 1595. They were eventually published by Thorpe in 1609.

There are 154 sonnets. The first 126 relate to Henry Wriothesly, the next 26 relate to Shakespeare's affair with the Dark Lady, probably Emilia Lanier, and the last two concern his visit to Bath, to rid himself of 'love's distemper.' The first sequence has a further sequence embedded in it which concerns Wriothesly's affair with another poet, probably Christopher Marlowe.

The story in the Sonnets reads like an Elizabethan soap opera, if they are read as a whole rather than piecemeal, as is the practice in far too many schools. Briefly, Shakespeare and Wriothesly were good friends, as well as poet and patron. Probably under the urgings of Wriothesly's family, many of the early poems are attempts to convince the young Earl to settle down and produce an heir, often by pointing out how mortal even the most beautiful and lively youth was. The very first line of the first poem is 'From fairest creature's we desire increase.' In Sonnet 20 there is direct reference to the femininity of Wriothesly and that, while Shakespeare loves him, he does not share his gender preference. The poems continue from there to praise his Lordship, through the waxing and waning of his favour, occasionally chiding him, but always declaring affection.

At Sonnet 78, there is a clear declaration that another poet has entered Wriothesly's affections, one who Shakespeare acknowledges in 79 to be a better poet than himself. This is almost certainly Marlowe. Poet, dramatist, academic and possibly a secret agent for the Queen, Marlowe was a man of great charisma and one who had a preference for other men. By Sonnet 87, we see that Shakespeare has all but given up on the Earl and a few of the following poems seem to be warning him that he's in dangerous company.

Marlowe was killed in a tavern brawl, possibly by a hired agent, and Sonnet 97 celebrates Shakespeare's return to Wriothesly's favour. The sonnets after this point, while still in praise, seem somehow more serious, culminating in one of the most beautiful of all the sonnets, 116: 'Do not to the marriage of true minds/ admit impediments - - -.'

When we arrive at the Sonnets to Emilia Lanier, we find Shakespeare praising her dark beauty, in contrast to the fashion of the day, which was for fair hair and pale skin. Lanier, however, was of Italian descent and had dark hair and olive complexion. The affair was not one which was easy, though. Lanier was a manipulative woman with an eye for the main chance and took advantage of an introduction to Wriothesly to begin an affair with him. After all, he was younger, had more money and was single. Sonnet 144 shows plainly how Shakespeare was caught in the middle of the affair and how Lanier tempts Wriothesly, dumping Shakespeare. But, as is ever the case, Shakespeare cannot simply turn and walk away but continues his words to her up to 152, when there is a clear break.

The last two Sonnets describe the journey to Bath, to take the waters. He hopes that this will cure him of his feelings for Lanier, who by now has been dumped by Wriothesly. She returned to her husband, a court musician who was actually known and liked by the Earl, more than he liked her, it seems.

Because of the way in which the Sonnets are intimately involved with Shakespeare's life, they are more felt, more from the heart, than the longer poems. There are few, if any, sonnet cycles in any language which can match their strength, and the best of them are simply among the best poetry ever written in English.

Verdict: 5/5, with a bullet.

Reference Materials

Books

The Re-Imagined Text: Shakespeare, Adaptation, & Eighteenth-Century Literary Theory; Jean I Marsden, University Press of Kentucky, Lexington, 1995.

Shakespeare's Defence Of Poetry: A Midsummer Night's Dream And The Tempest; Diana Akers Roads, University Press of America, Lanham MD, 1985.

Shakespeare's Theory Of Drama; Pauline Kiernan, Cambridge University Press, Cambridge and New York, 1996.

Shakespeare And The Rhetoricians; Marion Trousdale, University of North Carolina Press, Chapel Hill, 1982.

A Companion To Shakespeare; David Scott Kasten (ed), Blackwell Publishers, Oxford, 1999.

Discovering Shakespeare: A Chapter In Literary History; A L Rowse, Weidenfeld, London, 1989.

On Directing Shakespeare: Interviews With Contemporary Directors; Ralph Berry, Hamish Hamilton, London, 1989.

Political Shakespeare: Essays In Cultural Materialism; Jonathan Dollimore and Alan Sinfield (eds), Manchester University Press, Manchester, 1994.

Shakespeare: A Dramatic Life; Stanley Wells, Sinclair–Stevenson, London, 1994.

The Shakespeare Conspiracy; Graham Phillips and Martin Keatman, Century, London, 1994.

Shakespeare In His Context: The Constellated Globe; M C Bradbrook, Harvester Wheatsheaf, Hemel Hempstead, 1989.

Shakespeare The Aesthete: An Exploration Of Literary Theory; Lachlan Mackinnion, Macmillan, London, 1988.

Shakespeare: The Evidence: Unlocking The Mysteries Of The Man And His Work; Ian Wilson, Headline, London, 1993.

Shakespeare A To Z: The Essential Reference To His Plays, His Poems, His Life And Times, And More; Charles Boyce, Facts on File, New York, 1990.

The Essential Shakespeare: An Annotated Bibliography Of Major Modern Studies; Larry S Champion, G K Hall & Co, New York, 1993.

The Hutchinson Shakespeare Dictionary: An A –Z Guide To Shakespeare's Plays, Characters And Contemporaries; Sandra Clark (ed), Arrow Books, London, 1991.

Shakespeare And The Moving Image: The Plays On Film And Television; Anthony Davies and Stanley Wells (eds), Cambridge University Press, Cambridge, 1994.

The Shakespeare Handbook; Levi Fox (ed), Hall, Boston, 1987.

A Dictionary Of Shakespeare's Sexual Puns And Their Significance; Frankie Rubinstein, Macmillan, Basingstoke, 1989.

The Harvard Concordance To Shakespeare; Marvin Spevack, Harvard University Press, Cambridge, Mass., 1973.

A Shakespeare Thesaurus; Marvin Spevack, G Olms, Hildesheim, 1993.

Shakespeare In The Public Records; David Thomas, H M S O, London, 1985.

The Cambridge Companion To Shakespeare Studies; Stanley Wells, Cambridge University Press, Cambridge, 1987.

Shakespeare: An Illustrated Dictionary; Stanley Wells, Oxford University Press, Oxford, 1985.

A Dictionary Of Shakespeare; Stanley Wells, Oxford University Press, Oxford, 1998.

A Dictionary Of Shakespeare's Semantic Wordplay; Gilian West, Edwin Mellen Press, Lewiston, 1998.

A Dictionary Of Sexual Language And Imagery In Shakespearean And Stuart Literature; Gordon Williams, Athlone Press, London, 1994.

Shakespeare's Dramatic Structures; Anthony Brennan, Routledge, London, 1988.

Shakespeare's Life And Stage; S H Burton, Chambers, Edinburgh, 1989.

Shakespeare's Professional Career; Peter Thompson, Cambridge University Press, Cambridge, 1994.

Tragic Partnership In Shakespeare's Plays; University College of Swansea, Swansea, 1988.

William Shakespeare: The Anatomy Of An Enigma; Peter Razzell, Caliban, London, 1990.

Shakespeare: A Study And Research Guide; David M Bergeron, Saint Martin's Press, New York, 1975.

Journals

Shakespeare Quarterly; Folger Shakespeare Library, Washington. (quarterly)

Shakespeare Survey; Cambridge University Press, Cambridge. (annual)

Websites

The Complete Works of William Shakespeare - http://the-tech.mit.edu:80/Shakespeare/works.html

The Oxford Shakespeare - http://education.yahoo.com/reference/shakespeare/

World Shakespeare bibliography online - www-english.tamu.edu/wsb/

Shakespeare on screen - http://www.folger.edu/institute/visual/sh_pathfinder.htm

Mr William Shakespeare and the Internet - http://daphne.palomar.edu/shakespeare/

Webspeare - http://cncn.com/homepages/ken_m/shakespeare.html

Bartleby.com - http://www.bartleby.com/reference/

University of Virginia Library - http://etext.lib.virginia.edu/shakespeare/

Edhelper.com - http://www.edhelper.com/shakespeare.htm

About.com: Shakespeare - http://shakespeare.about.com/

The Essential Library: Currently Available

Film Directors:

Woody Allen (2nd)	Tim Burton	Ang Lee
Jane Campion*	John Carpenter	Joel & Ethan Coen (2nd)
Jackie Chan	Steve Soderbergh	Clint Eastwood
David Cronenberg	Terry Gilliam*	Michael Mann
Alfred Hitchcock (2nd)	Krzysztof Kieslowski*	Roman Polanski
Stanley Kubrick (2nd)	Sergio Leone	Oliver Stone
David Lynch	Brian De Palma*	George Lucas
Sam Peckinpah*	Ridley Scott (2nd)	James Cameron
Orson Welles (2nd)	Billy Wilder	
Steven Spielberg	Mike Hodges	

Film Genres:

Blaxploitation Films	Bollywood	French New Wave
Horror Films	Spaghetti Westerns	Vietnam War Movies
Slasher Movies	Film Noir	German Expresionist Films
Vampire Films*	Heroic Bloodshed*	

Film Subjects:

Laurel & Hardy	Marx Brothers	Film Music
Steve McQueen*	Marilyn Monroe	The Oscars® (2nd)
Filming On A Microbudget	Bruce Lee	Writing A Screenplay

TV:

Doctor Who

Literature:

Cyberpunk	Philip K Dick	The Beat Generation
Agatha Christie	Sherlock Holmes	Noir Fiction*
Terry Pratchett	Hitchhiker's Guide (2nd)	Alan Moore
William Shakespeare		

Ideas:

Conspiracy Theories	Nietzsche	UFOs
Feminism	Freud & Psychoanalysis	Bisexuality

History:

Alchemy & Alchemists	The Crusades	The Black Death
Jack The Ripper	The Rise Of New Labour	Ancient Greece
American Civil War	American Indian Wars	

Miscellaneous:

The Madchester Scene	Stock Market Essentials	Beastie Boys
How To Succeed As A Sports Agent		
How To Succeed In The Music Business		

Available at all good bookstores or send a cheque (payable to 'Oldcastle Books') to: **Pocket Essentials (Dept WSH), 18 Coleswood Rd, Harpenden, Herts, AL5 1EQ, UK**. £3.99 each (£2.99 if marked with an *). For each book add 50p postage & packing in the UK and £1 elsewhere.